Reclaiming Social Work

Challenging Neo-liberalism and Promoting Social Justice

Iain Ferguson

SAGE Publications
Los Angeles • London • New Delhi • Singapore

First published 2008

SAGE Publications Ltd
1 Oliver's Yard
55 City Road
London EC1Y 1SP

SAGE Publications Inc.
2455 Teller Road
Thousand Oaks, California 91320

SAGE Publications India Pvt Ltd
B 1/I 1 Mohan Cooperative Industrial Area
Mathura Road
New Delhi 110 044

SAGE Publications Asia-Pacific Pte Ltd
33 Pekin Street #02-01
Far East Square
Singapore 048763

Library of Congress Control Number: 2007927366

British Library Cataloguing in Publication data

A catalogue record for this book is available from the British Library

ISBN 978–1–4129–0692–0
ISBN 978–1–4129–0693–7 (pbk)

Typeset by Newgen Imaging Systems (P) Ltd, Chennai, India
Printed in India at Replika Press Pvt. Ltd
Printed on paper from sustainable resources

Contents

Acknowledgements

Inevitably, a book of this sort is a collective production, in that it draws on the work of many other critical writers, notably Chris Jones, John Harris and Alex Callinicos, as well as countless conversations over the years with friends, colleagues and comrades too numerous to mention with whom I have been involved in a host of socialist and campaigning movements. My thanks to all of them.

Thanks are also due to Anna Luker and Zoë Elliot-Fawcett at Sage who have been a marvellous source of support throughout, and who have shown infinite patience and understanding when it came to re-negotiating deadlines.

Three special mentions are necessary. First of all, I have gained a huge amount from the friendship of Mike Gonzalez over more than thirty years. His creative, resolutely non-sectarian understanding of Marxism, coupled with an apparently inexhaustible enthusiasm for the struggle, has influenced and inspired me enormously, as it has the thousands of others who have benefited from his talks and writings over the years on every aspect of socialist theory, culture and history. In the wake of the loss of his partner Clare after a very long illness, I wish to put on record my thanks and appreciation to him.

Second, this book began life as a collaboration with Michael Lavalette. Unfortunately, the demands of life as a local councillor for the Respect Coalition in Preston, while holding down a full-time job as a Senior Lecturer in Social Policy at Liverpool University, meant that something had to give, and in this case, it was the book. Nevertheless, many of the ideas and arguments which follow grew out of discussions with Michael and earlier publications in which we were jointly involved, so thanks also to him.

Finally, Dorte, my partner, has had to tolerate long periods during the writing of this book when I was present in body only. Despite this, she has constantly encouraged me to complete the book and been prepared to be bored to death as I ran yet another draft chapter by her. Between her own commitments as a mental health service manager and a creative glass artist, she has always found time to give support, suggestions and ideas. Love and many, many thanks are due to her.

Some chapters in this book draw on previous publications. Thanks are due to Oxford Journals (Oxford University Press) for kind permission to draw on 'Increasing user choice or privatizing risk? The antinomies of personalization', *British Journal of Social Work* 2007, 37(3): 387–403 (Chapter 5). Thanks are also due to Sage Publications for permission to draw on 'Living in a material world: Postmodernism and social policy' in M. Lavalette and A. Pratt (eds) (2005) *Social Policy: A Conceptual and Theoretical Introduction*, 3rd edn, London Sage (Chapter 7). Parts of Chapter 8 first appeared in Ferguson, I. and Lavalette, M. (2006) 'Globalization and global justice: Towards a social work of resistance', *International Social Work*, 49(3): 309–18 and again thanks are due to Sage Publications. Finally the arguments on 'the science of happiness' in Chapter 8 were first put forward in a paper entitled 'An Attitude Problem? Mental Health, Inequality and the "Science of Happiness"', delivered at the Glasgow School of Social Work on 10 November 2006 as part of an ESRC-funded Social Work and Health Inequalities Research Seminar Series. I am grateful to the organisers of the series for inviting me to participate and to those present for their helpful feedback.

Introduction

In August 2006, along with other British social work academics, I was fortunate enough to attend the International Association of Schools of Social Work Conference in Santiago, Chile. The Conference was memorable for many reasons. The keynote speech at the opening ceremony, for example, was given by the recently elected President of Chile, Michelle Bachelet. Bachelet's presence at the Conference was powerful and symbolic, not so much because of her politics (which are less radical than those of other Latin American leaders like Evo Morales and Hugo Chavez), nor solely because she is the first woman to hold the office of president in Chile (though in a continent where notions of *machismo* are still influential, this is no mean feat). Rather, Bachelet's presence was particularly powerful because she is a survivor. Like many thousands of others, she, her mother and her father suffered horribly at the hands of the Pinochet dictatorship which overthrew the democratically elected government of Salvador Allende on 11 September 1973. All three were held at the notorious torture centre, the Villa Grimaldi, on the outskirts of Santiago. While she and her mother were released after an ordeal involving horrors which one can only imagine, her father, a navy admiral who was loyal to the elected government, died, like many others, at the hands of the torturers. When Bachelet spoke, therefore, about the importance of the social work profession and the struggle for human rights, there was an awareness amongst those present that this was no empty politician's rhetoric but that she was speaking from first-hand experience, both of the suffering she experienced and of the help she received.

Also memorable were the Conference contributions from the Latin American delegates. For several years, Latin America has been at the forefront of the global struggle against neo-liberalism, the ideology which tells us that everything – public services, the environment, life itself – should be subordinated to the requirements of the market and big business. That experience of struggle was reflected in many of the papers from Latin American social workers and social work academics, both in their willingness to employ the language of a radical Marxism (with the ideas of the Hungarian philosopher George Lukacs underpinning several contributions) and in their attempts to make connections between social work and the social movements in recent years, including the Landless Workers' Movement (MST) in Brazil, and the Piquiteros movement in Argentina.

For some of us, however, the most moving part of the whole week came on the final day, with a Human Rights trip organised by the Chilean Association of Social Workers. This began with a guided tour of the Villa Grimaldi, now a Garden of Remembrance to victims of the dictatorship. It continued to the small rural town of Paine where the thirty or so delegates met with the families of the seventy-nine local men who had 'disappeared' following the coup, due in part to their involvement in the land reforms introduced by the Allende government. The trip ended at the headquarters of the Chilean Association of Social Workers. Here, the walls are lined with photographs of (mainly young) social workers who had 'disappeared' or had been murdered by the military, with each room in the headquarters named after one of those who died that way. Social workers, the President of the Association explained, were particularly distrusted by the regime and a disproportionate number of them were tortured or murdered. In addition, social work education was downgraded during the years of the dictatorship and only recently has it become once more a university-based profession.

The experience of social workers under the Pinochet dictatorship was, thankfully, an exceptional one and in most respects, very different from the experience of most social workers in the liberal democracies of the West, where the risk of stress-related burnout is a more common occupational hazard than the risk of violence, imprisonment or torture. Nevertheless, the experience of those Chilean social workers connects with the current experience of social workers in Britain and elsewhere in two important ways. First, while 'Thatcherism' in Britain and 'Reaganomics' in the USA are often thought of as the first attempts to implement economic policies that opened up every area of life and society to market forces, in fact, as Susan George reminds us, the real test-bed of neo-liberalism was Chile. It was there, under the ideal conditions of the Pinochet dictatorship, that the group of economists known as the 'Chicago Boys' because they had taken their degrees at the most neo-liberal university economics department in the USA, swung into action, opening up the whole economy to privatisation, removing all social safety nets and impoverishing huge numbers of people (George, 2004: 20).

Since then, neo-liberalism has become the 'common sense' of most governments throughout the world, whether the ruling party is right-wing and conservative or, as in Britain, a Labour (or social democratic) Party whose role in former times was seen as being to defend working-class people from the harmful effects of these very same market forces. The promise of neo-liberalism was that it would create a more prosperous society, not only for those at the top, but also, as a result of wealth 'trickling down', for those at the bottom. In fact, as I shall argue in the early chapters of this book, the pursuit of neo-liberal policies in Britain, first under

Conservative governments and, since 1997, under New Labour, has created a much more unequal society, in which the lives of millions (including millions of children) are still blighted by poverty.

While those who rely on State-provided welfare services have suffered most as a result of such policies, neo-liberalism has also profoundly transformed the jobs of those who provide such services and the organisations in which they work. As Harris has shown in his important study of the 'social work business' in Britain, every aspect of social work has been profoundly affected by the imposition of a culture of managerialism and competition over the past decade and a half (Harris, 2003). As recent government-funded reports have shown, one consequence of that culture has been to create a profound dissatisfaction amongst social workers over what their jobs have become, a sense of a growing gap between their day-to-day tasks and the values which brought them into the job in the first place (Scottish Executive, 2006a).

Some flavour of how far that managerial culture has moved social work from its original aims and ideals can be gleaned from the following e-mail flyer sent out to social work staff by the trade journal *careandhealth* in March 2007, advertising its forthcoming training programme for managers:

2007 Is The Year For Advanced Performance Management

If you have not been trained in the latest advances in *Time Compression* and *Waste Elimination*, or if the words *Kaizen, Gemba,* and *Kanban* are unfamiliar, you need to re-tool your management skills to meet the demands of the next phase of service delivery. The Certificate in Advanced Performance Management' equips senior managers with the skills to achieve radical and tangible advances in the performance management of their organisations.

I am writing to remind you about *CareandHealth's* upcoming Management Training course – The Certificate in Advanced Performance Management – that will be commencing in a few weeks, so book now to ensure your place. This City & Guilds and CIPFA accredited course has been specifically designed to meet the needs of senior managers charged with leading the performance improvement of their organisations and sets new standards in developing performance management in health and social care. It will provide you with intensive and demanding training in leading edge tools and techniques that have proven success in world class organisations. Integrates Lean and Six Sigma with powerful new methodologies specifically tailored for the UK health and social care sector. This advanced course has been designed specifically for high-level experienced managers with the vision to achieve rapid service improvement and the drive to acquire the skills necessary to affect it. The course is open to experienced, senior performance managers wishing to further their skills with the latest advances, as well as those who have previously completed and passed *Care and Health's* Certificate in Performance Management course. After an intensive immersion in the latest tools and techniques, you will stand out amongst your peers. (www.careandhealth.com)

Brave New World that has such managers in it!

Paradoxically, however, as I shall argue in this book, in the dissatisfaction that this managerial culture has bred lie the seeds of hope for the future of social work, as well as the second point of connection with those Chilean social workers. For despite the ways in which social work in the UK and elsewhere has been undermined over the past twenty years, and castigated by government and media as a 'failing' profession, the belief that a concern for human rights should be at the core of social work and that social workers should be on the side of the poor and the oppressed, remains strong throughout the global social work community. It is a belief reflected, for example, in the influential definition of social work suggested by the International Federation of Social Workers (www.ifsw.org.com.) and one which is present, if often unacknowledged, in the day-to-day practice of many workers. In addition, as Cree and Davis have shown in their study of the views of social workers, service users and carers in the UK, the desire to 'make a difference', both to the lives of individuals and to the society in which we live, remains the main motivating factor for becoming a social worker (Cree and Davis, 2007). It is, above all, the frustration of these hopes, beliefs and desires by ideologies and policies which insist that the primary role of social workers is to 'manage' 'high-risk' families or individuals, to ration increasingly meagre services, and to collude in the demonisation of groups such as young people and asylum seekers which is giving rise to current discontent. Neo-liberalism in social work, in other words, is creating resistance. Moreover, since managerial policies undermine *all* forms of social work practice and values, 'traditional' as well as 'radical' or 'emancipatory', it is a dissatisfaction and a resistance which goes well beyond the ranks of a small number of politically committed individuals and embraces very large numbers of workers who might not think of themselves as 'political'.

That resistance has also been fuelled and reinforced by the emergence of two types of social movement. First, there have been social welfare movements such as the disability movement and the mental health users' movement which have challenged traditional models of relationships and services and which have also, in recent years, been at the forefront of the struggle against government attempts to reduce welfare spending. More significant in terms of overall impact, however, has been the global movement against neo-liberalism – the anti-capitalist or global justice movement – which has developed since the turn of the century and whose central slogan, that 'The world is not a commodity!', reflects the widespread feeling amongst many social workers that their practice should be driven by values of respect and social justice, rather than budgetary considerations (Ferguson and Lavalette, 2004). As I shall argue in Chapter 6, in the past, social work's commitment to social justice and social change has been strengthened through its contact with wider social movements. In the same way, social workers today can draw on the wider resistance to the domination of every aspect of life by money to recreate new forms of practice, while also re-discovering its own radical past.

These factors, then – dissatisfaction with what social work has become, the rise of new movements of service users and their allies, and the emergence of new global movements against neo-liberalism and war – are the 'resources of hope' which were initially identified by some of us in the Social Work Manifesto in 2004 (Jones et al., 2004), and out of which, as I shall argue in this book, a new engaged practice, rooted in social justice, can emerge.

Structure of the Book

In Chapter 1, I argue that, despite Conservative hostility and New Labour ambivalence, social work has not only survived into the twenty-first century but has actually expanded, both in Britain and internationally. As radical critics foresaw, however, it has often done so in the form of a neo-liberal social work which places budgets and managerial priorities above social work values. This chapter begins the discussion of the possibilities for a different kind of social work, rooted in social justice, through consideration both of the new movements against neo-liberalism and war which have emerged in recent years, and through identifying some elements of the 'radical kernel' which have been present in social work since its inception.

Chapter 2 explores the promise and reality of the ideology which, for most of the past two decades, has been the common sense of governments throughout the world, regardless of the political party in power: neo-liberalism. Focusing mainly on the experience in Britain under New Labour since 1997, I shall examine the ways in which neo-liberal policies (often wrapped up in the language of the 'Third Way') have impacted on poverty, inequality and insecurity, categories which most users of social work services know only too well.

In Chapter 3 , the focus narrows to explore the roots of New Labour's oft-noted ambivalence to social work, and to examine the specific ways in which governments under former prime minister Tony Blair have sought to make professional social work 'fit for purpose'. On the one hand, this will involve discussion of the ways in which the moral authoritarianism underpinning New Labour policies in areas such as youth justice and asylum clash with core social work values, on the other, consideration of three key elements of the modernisation agenda: managerialism, regulation and evidence-based practice.

A core objective of the NHS and Community Care Act 1990 was the creation of a market in care, with the private sector playing a greatly increased role. Through consideration of the voluntary (or Third) sector, the private sector and individualised budgets in the form of direct payments, Chapter 4 explores the ways in which the provision of social care has been transformed since the early 1990s, and critically assesses the neo-liberal assumption that competition between service providers is the best guarantor of high-quality services.

It is now common in discussions of service user involvement to distinguish between top-down, consumerist models, on the one hand, and democratic models, often associated with collective service user movements, on the other. In the first half of Chapter 5, I shall critically assess the argument, propounded by John Harris amongst others, that the potential of consumerist models for service user empowerment (or social development) has been understated. In the second half of Chapter 6, through discussion of the contribution made by the mental health service users' movement in the areas of worker/user relationships, new services and policy and legislative change, I shall suggest that it is to the collective discussions and activities of such service user movements that we should look in the first instance for ideas and strategies which can contribute to the development of genuinely empowering practice and services.

Chapter 6 explores the radical tradition in social work. While often identified exclusively with the movement which developed in Britain, Australia and Canada in the early 1970s, I shall show, drawing on examples from early British social work and from American social work in the first half of the twentieth century, that radicalism in social work has a much longer history. That said, the 1970s radical social work movement was of particular significance and the second half of this chapter will be given over to an assessment of its ideas and activities, as well as its legacy for social workers today. A core concern of this chapter will be to highlight the ways in which social work in the past has often been radicalised by social movements in the wider society.

One element of that legacy has been the emergence since the 1990s of critical social work, particularly in Australia and Canada. In Chapter 7, I shall discuss two models of critical social work: a *broad* model which, while critical of what it sees as radical social work's overemphasis on class and underemphasis on oppression, nevertheless, like its radical predecessor, recognisably belongs to a tradition with roots in modernist or Enlightenment assumptions; and a *narrow* model, based mainly on the ideas of postmodernism. While acknowledging the commitment of critical social work theorists of all hues to challenging oppression, I shall suggest that postmodernism fails to provide social work with a clear foundation for doing so.

Chapter 8 explores the ways in which growing opposition to the neo-liberal consensus of the past two decades is opening up spaces for the development of new, engaged forms of social work practice. One aspect of that opposition, albeit as I shall show a rather limited one, is the 'Happiness' movement which has emerged in recent years and whose central tenet is that consumerism does not provide a basis for satisfying living. Much more significant is the anti-capitalist or global justice movement, already referred to in Chapter 1. That movement, and its central assertion that 'The world is not a commodity!' finds a strong echo from within a social work profession shaped much more by budgets and competition rather than by core values. Dissatisfaction with the dominance of financial and managerial priorities is, I shall argue, creating widespread resistance across very broad layers of social workers. If that dissatisfaction can be given voice and organisation, it may yet become an important resource in the creation of a different form of social work, rooted in social justice and more able to address the poverty, inequality and oppression which continue to be the lot of a majority of service users in the twenty-first century.

1

A Profession Worth Fighting For?

Introduction: After Social Work?

Throughout much of the world, the 1980s were tough years for those involved in fighting for social justice and social change. The 1960s and early 1970s had seen the emergence in many countries of powerful new social movements, against war in Vietnam and for the liberation of women, gays and black people, coupled with a resurgent trade union movement in Britain, France and elsewhere. The rise of these movements had led many to believe that real social and political change was on the global agenda (Harman, 1988; Kurlansky, 2004). In contrast, the 1980s saw the old ruling order re-establish itself in Britain, the USA and elsewhere, through the vehicle of a new, aggressive neo-liberalism (Harvey, 2005). There was, of course, still resistance, both internationally and in Britain. Whether it was workers in Poland fighting to establish *Solidarnosc* – the biggest trade union in the world – in the early 1980s, the campaign against Margaret Thatcher's hated poll tax at the end of the decade, or the magnificent, and ultimately successful, struggle of trade unionists and activists in South Africa to overthrow the brutal apartheid regime, people continued to fight for change. Yet in the main, the social and political struggles of these years were often bitter and defensive attempts to hang on to some of the gains made during earlier periods, whether in the form of trade union rights or a woman's right to control her own body.

More than any other health or welfare profession, social work suffered from the shift in the political climate during these years. In the 1970s, social workers in Britain and elsewhere had begun to break from the narrow, individualised and often pathologising focus which had characterised much social work practice till then. The 1980s, in contrast, was a period of retreat. As the decade progressed, a combination of factors which included the rise of mass unemployment, a financial squeeze on social work spending and a hostile government and media intent on portraying social work as a 'failing profession' combined to reduce the scope for progressive practice (Clarke, 1993). Again there was resistance, and even some progress in social work education in the areas of anti-racist and anti-oppressive practice (albeit of an increasingly 'top-down' nature and within a narrow context of regulation and control – Penketh, 2000; Langan, 2002). The growth of managerialism (or New Public Management), however, from the late 1980s onwards, underpinning the extension of market forces into social work, further squeezed the potential of social work to act as a force for social change and added to a sense of alienation amongst many front-line workers (Clarke and Newman, 1997; McDonald, 2006).

Given this climate, it is hardly surprising that a mood of despondency and pessimism should occasionally have affected some of those who earlier had been in the forefront of the development of more radical social work approaches. Jones and Novak, for example, writing in the *British Journal of Social Work* in 1993, suggested that

> It would appear that until the political climate changes and there is a widespread revulsion against current trends and inequalities, social work might continue as an occupation but perish as a caring and liberal profession. (Jones and Novak, 1993: 211)

Further into the 1990s, Clarke, in a paper entitled 'After Social Work?' reflected on the ways in which managerialism and marketisation were fragmenting both social work organisations and the social work task, and posed the questions:

> How can one struggle over what a 'client-centered' social work would look like when the client has been abolished and replaced by 'a customer'? How can commitments to 'anti-discriminatory practice' be articulated within a managerial agenda which is dominated by the quest for efficiency? The old points of leverage have been marginalised, to be replaced by corporate visions, competition and confusion. That multi-faceted dislocation matters both for those who practise social work and those who receive it. For both, the future looks bleaker after social work. (Clarke, 1996: 60)

Clarke's paper was extremely prescient. The intensification of managerialism under New Labour governments since 1997 has indeed meant that many social workers in the UK do now work in organisations with managers who have no background or training in social work. In the interests of 'joint working' and 'integrated services', social work departments have often been merged with other local authority departments, such as housing, and in some cases have been closed down altogether, with staff relocated into departments of education or health. The growth of the social care sector and the increasing individualisation of services is contributing to the process of de-professionalisation, both within the voluntary sector (or Third Sector, as it is now usually referred to) and within local authorities. Others, meantime, are relocated into call centres owned by private multinational companies like BT.

Yet despite these changes, and despite a profound ambivalence and distrust towards social workers on the part of New Labour which has led to their exclusion from key welfare programmes (Jordan with Jordan, 2000), the profession has not disappeared, either in Britain or elsewhere. On the contrary, on a global scale, as Lorenz has noted:

> Social work is very much in demand, enjoys a boom, represents a growth industry even in countries that ideologically would rather do without it. (Lorenz, 2005a: 97)

In part, this expansion is itself a reflection of these same political and economic processes discussed above – national, European and global – which are aimed at creating greater integration of markets and increased government regulation of professional education and practice (Penna, 2004). In the UK, for example, an expansion of social work education has resulted in part from the Bologna process of harmonising European social work education, which means that social work in the UK is now a graduate profession (Lorenz, 2005b). In addition, the development of new forms of governance under New Labour has given rise to a raft of new social work bodies, including the Social Care Councils, the Commissions on Social Care, the Social Care Institute for Excellence and its Scottish equivalent. In Scotland, *Changing Lives*, the Report of a major enquiry into social work commissioned by the Scottish Executive, is likely to give rise to major legislative changes, creating a new framework for the profession for the coming period (Scottish Executive, 2006a). Meanwhile, as noted by Lorenz, on a global scale it does appear that social work in one form or other is seen by governments as having a role to play within advanced market societies. The fact that social work schools are springing up rapidly in the newly marketised societies of Eastern Europe, and also China, suggests that the governments of these countries see a use for professional social work in situations of growing social and economic inequality and dislocation (Yip, 2007). It seems likely, then, that social work will survive, though the fact that it will often do so in a truncated and sometimes punitive form means that in itself, this is hardly a cause for celebration.

More importantly, however, in terms of the *form* in which social work survives, there has been a second development in the years since these articles were written which gives grounds for genuine hope, since in important respects it represents the beginnings of the 'widespread revulsion against current trends and inequalities' which Jones and Novak saw as the basis for social work's re-emergence as a liberal, humane profession. The late 1990s saw the emergence of a powerful reaction against the neo-liberal version of globalisation which had become the common sense of most governments, both conservative and social-democratic, during that decade. For much of the past two decades, as the radical journalist George Monbiot observed, the great advantage of the neo-liberals had been that they had only one idea: that society should subordinate all other concerns to the interests of big business (Monbiot, 2001: 5). It was that idea above all, however, that came under attack at the end of the decade. The turning-point in the development of opposition to neo-liberalism, the 'fork in the road' as the American anti-corporate campaigner Ralph Nader described it, came in the city of Seattle in November, 1999. There, 40,000 demonstrators, drawn from a very wide variety of constituencies, brought the proceedings of the World Trade Organisation to a halt and, in doing so, initiated a global movement which has since challenged neo-liberal governments and neo-liberal policies on every continent (Charlton, 2000; Danaher, 2001). Joseph Stiglitz, Nobel Prize-winner and former Chief Economist at the World Bank, and a critic of the dominant version of globalisation, has explained the significance of this new movement:

> Until the protestors came along, there was little hope for change and no outlet for complaints. *Some* of the protestors went to excesses; *some* of the protestors were arguing for higher protectionist barriers against the developing countries which would have made their plight even worse. But despite these problems, it is the trade unionists, students, environmentalists – ordinary citizens – who have put the need for reform on the agenda of the developed world. (Stiglitz, 2002: 9)

In the years which followed Seattle, this anti-capitalist movement (or global justice movement, as it is sometimes called) has grown and developed in four different, though connected, ways. First, there have been the demonstrations. Since 1999, each time the world's business and government elites, notably the World Trade Organisation and the G8 group of world leaders, have met to discuss ways in which the liberalisation agenda can be taken a stage further, their deliberations have taken place against the background of large mobilisations by angry protestors, drawn overwhelmingly from the country in which they are meeting (Callinicos, 2003). More than 300,000 protestors, for example, gathered in Edinburgh, Scotland in July 2005 to demand that the G8 leaders meeting in nearby Gleneagles 'make poverty history' (Hubbard and Miller, 2005).

Second, the movement has developed its own structures and discussion points in the form of the World Social Forum and Regional Social Forums, where the experiences of opposition to the free-market policies of the G8 and WTO can be shared and alternative policies proposed and debated. Since 2001 such gatherings, typically involving tens of thousands of participants, have regularly taken place in cities across the globe including Porto Alegre, Cairo, Mumbai, Florence, Paris and London (George, 2004).

Third, the influence of this movement, coupled with people's direct experience of neo-liberal policies, has fuelled mass movements against privatisation in many different countries and contributed directly and indirectly to political change. This is most obviously the case in Latin America, where struggles against the privatisation of basic utilities such as water and electricity have given rise to huge popular movements in countries like Colombia and Ecuador and elsewhere, as in Venezuela and Bolivia, that have led to the election of new radical governments (Ali, 2006). Meanwhile in Europe, opposition to the neo-liberal agenda has led to the creation of new political parties which, in several countries including Italy, Portugal, Britain and Germany, have gained parliamentary representation.

Finally, since 2003, the movement has been central to the development of an even bigger global social movement in opposition to the devastating wars in Iraq and Afghanistan (as well as the ongoing occupation of Palestine by the Israeli state). Following the events of 9/11 in New York in 2001, there was a widespread assumption, voiced by the *New York Times*, that the global justice movement would wither away, unable to withstand the patriotic fervour engendered by George W. Bush's 'war on terrorism'. Instead, the movement rapidly developed in an anti-war direction, with many people easily making the connection between the economic policies of the world's most powerful states and corporations and their military policies, summed up in the popular slogan 'No blood for oil'. The result has been the biggest anti-war movement the world has ever seen, with 10 million people marching globally on 15 February 2003, including 2 million people on the streets of London (Murray and German, 2005). One indication of the extent to which this movement has shaped popular consciousness is the fact that the term 'imperialism', long associated with some of the more esoteric sects on the far left, has once again become a term of common use in describing the behaviour of the major powers. As one prominent critic of the wars of recent years has noted:

> I used not to use the word imperialism. I thought young people wouldn't even know what it meant. Then Robert Cooper [formerly foreign policy adviser to Blair] writes a pamphlet in which he openly calls for what he describes as a new imperialism. Suddenly I find that everyone is using the words imperialism and anti-imperialism and I think that is a jolly good thing. If something looks like a duck and walks like a duck, the chances are it is a duck. That's exactly what we've got going now – a new imperialism. All sides are using its real name. (Galloway, 2003: 117)

Challenging Neo-liberal Social Work

What might be the significance of this global movement, and this shift in popular consciousness, for those seeking to recreate a social work profession rooted in notions of social justice? First, without understating the extent to which neo-liberal ideas and policies continue to dominate the political landscape in Britain and in many other countries, the movement has been successful in challenging the notion that neo-liberal globalisation is the only show in town. One indication of the shift in ideas that has taken place is that some of those who, less than a decade ago, were arguing that social democratic governments need not concern themselves overmuch with issues of inequality are now to be found arguing for a 'new egalitarianism' (Giddens and Diamond, 2005).

Second, as Thompson has argued (Thompson, 2002), social work in the past has been profoundly affected by its contact with social movements and the shifts in popular thinking which such movements bring about. This is most obviously true of Britain, Canada and Australia in the 1970s. In important respects, radical social work was a product of the great social movements of these years, notably the civil rights movement, the movement against the war in Vietnam, the women's movement and the struggles of trade unionists. On a smaller scale, in the 1980s and 1990s, 'new social welfare movements' such as the disability movement and the mental health users' movement have similarly exerted an influence on professional social work, reflected in the widespread acceptance of social models of disability and health. However, as I shall argue in Chapter 6, the links between social work and social movements go back much earlier than the 1970s and are not confined to the countries mentioned above. The ways in which the social movements of the twenty-first century – notably the anti-capitalist or global justice movement on the one hand and the anti-war movement on the other – can inform the development of a new, radical practice will be considered in Chapter 8.

Third, this wider dissatisfaction with neo-liberalism finds a strong echo from within a social work profession whose knowledge base, skills and values have been distorted and undermined by the imposition since the early 1990s of a pro-business ideology, sometimes referred to as New Public Management (NPM). McDonald identifies some of the key elements of NPM as being:

> a shift of focus by public sector leaders from policy to management; an emphasis on quantifiable performance measurements and appraisal, the break-up of traditional bureaucratic structures into quasi-autonomous units dealing with one another on a user-pays basis, market testing and competitive tendering instead of in-house provision, strong emphasis on cost-cutting, output targets rather than input controls, limited-term contracts for state employees instead of career tenure, monetized incentives rather than fixed salaries 'freedom to manage' instead of personnel control, more use of public relations and advertising and encouragement of self regulation instead of legislation. (McDonald, 2006: 69)

One of the main effects of these changes has been to hugely reduce the possibilities for social workers to undertake direct work with service users. The desire to 'work with people', alongside the aspiration to 'make a difference' have historically been amongst the main reasons for people coming into social work. Yet as *Changing Lives*, the Report of the 21st Century Social Work Review in Scotland published in 2006, makes clear it is precisely these aspects of the job that have been undermined by the changes described above:

> Working to achieve change is at the heart of what social workers do. Identifying needs and risks through assessment and developing and implementing action plans to address these will achieve nothing without an effective therapeutic relationship between worker and client ... Yet social workers consistently told us that it is this very aspect of their work which has been eroded and devalued in recent years under the pressure of workloads, increased bureaucracy and a more mechanistic and technical approach to delivering services. (Scottish Executive, 2006a: 28)

The social workers interviewed by Jones in one of the few studies to explore the experience of frontline social work in England in the year 2000 expressed very similar views:

> We are now much more office based. This really hit home the other day when the whole team was in the office working at their desks. We have loads more forms which take time to complete. But we social workers also do less and less direct work with clients. Increasingly the agency buys in other people to do the direct work and we manage it. (Jones, 2004: 100)

One factor underpinning this shift has been the reduction of professional social work to care management, reflecting the introduction of a purchaser/ provider split aimed at creating a market in social work and social care. Another factor creating worker dissatisfaction is the increasingly authoritarian climate in which workers are required to operate, particularly in the areas of asylum and youth justice. As another of Jones' respondents commented:

punitive

> I was talking to a youth justice worker last week and she told me how much she loved her job until the recent changes. Now she hates it as they do less work with kids, have got to be more concerned with disciplining them and have to work with police officers and the like. It seemed to her that it was all based around a punitive approach and that Jack Straw [Labour minister] was as bad as Michael Howard [Conservative Minister]. Both seem to hate youngsters and seem more concerned with criminalising the kids who are seen to be of no use. (Quoted in Jones, 2004: 103)

What is significant about this dissatisfaction is that it appears to affect much wider layers of social workers than those who were influenced by radical social work ideas in the 1970s. The reason is that neo-liberal social work, to use Jones's phrase, undermines not only radical or structural approaches but also 'traditional' relationship-based social work. The weakness of professional social work organisation in Britain and the failure (until recently) of the main social work trade union to seriously engage with these 'professional' issues means that the dissatisfaction and unhappiness which exists has until now usually been expressed in individualised ways – through sickness, moving job or leaving the profession.

In Chapter 8, however, we shall return to a discussion of the ways in which that dissatisfaction might be collectively channelled into the construction of a new engaged practice.

A Profession Worth Fighting for?

Both implicit and explicit in the arguments of these radical critics of current trends within social work is the view that the disappearance of a social work profession rooted in social justice would be a defeat for those committed to challenging oppression and inequality. Conversely, it would be an encouragement to those in positions of power who seek to blame the poor and oppressed for their own poverty and for the problems they experience (see also Jones et al., 2004). That view, it has to be said, is not a self-evident one. For much of its history, social work has been seen by the State – and experienced by those on the receiving end of social work services – primarily as a form of social control, with social workers the 'soft cops' who differ from 'hard cops' only in the technologies that they employ. At its most extreme, that social control remit over the past century has allowed for the involvement of social workers in Australia in the forced removal of Aboriginal children from their families and the placement of these children in white institutions or with white families (Briskman, 2003); social workers in 1930s Nazi Germany employing the transferable skills of 'assessment and counselling' to sort out those who were not seen as part of the nation's 'healthy stock' and helping them to 'come to terms emotionally with measures to which they had been subjected… i.e. institutionalisation, sterilisation or deportation' (Lorenz, 1994: 68); and closer to our own times, the expectation (and statutory requirement) that social workers in Britain will be involved in removing children from the families of asylum seekers who have been refused leave to remain (Hayes and Humphries, 2004). On a more day-to-day level, the statutory powers of social workers to remove children from their families, coupled with their roles of assessment, rationing of scarce resources and surveillance of poor families or 'risky' individuals means that they have frequently been viewed with fear and mistrust by the poorest sections of the population, and are seen in a much less positive light than other welfare professionals (Donzelot, 1980). Movies such as Ken Loach's *Ladybird, Ladybird* (1994), or Holman's collection of writings by parents in a deprived area of Glasgow highlight the ambivalence which many poor, working-class people feel towards social workers (Holman, 1998).

For much of its history, it is these controlling features of social work that have been to the fore. What is also true, however, is that historically, social work, to a greater extent than other health and social care professions has, from time to time, been an *awkward* or *troublesome* profession. It is a profession whose members have sometimes sided with their clients against the State and challenged dominant ideologies in a way that other professionals have not.

If social work is mistrusted by its clients, it is no less true that it has often been mistrusted by the State. In this respect, as Butler and Drakeford suggest, 'social work is heir to a radical, emancipatory and transformative ideal, or at least, it has the potential to promote such an ideal' (Butler and Drakeford, 2001: 16). Some sense of this potential for change is evident in the quote with which Cree and Davis end their 2007 study of service users' and workers' views of social work. For Sarah, a care-leaver who is about to begin her social work degree programme:

> I'm really passionate about social work – we *can* make a difference and inform practice and legislation. I know the difference social services made in my life, and I think I could do it, and do it really well. I know there's a lot of regulations and a lot of pressure – but I really want to do it and I think that I can make a difference. (Quoted in Cree and Davis, 2007: 159)

It is this 'radical kernel' of social work, the inherent tension between its controlling role on the one hand and its potential to be a force for social change and social justice on the other, that make social work different and social workers more than just 'soft cops'. In Chapter 6 I shall explore the nature and history of this radicalism in more detail. Here, however, I shall identify some of the elements which make social work, at least potentially, a troublesome profession and a profession worth fighting for.

A Site of Ideological Conflict

The most general explanation for the radicalism lurking within social work lies in its location within capitalist society. Since its inception, social work has acted as a prism which mirrors – and often distorts – the most fundamental divides and antagonisms of the society in which we live. Precisely because of the human material with which it deals, it is a site of ideological conflict. Its concern is to make sense of, and respond to, the ways in which human beings relate to each other as family members and as citizens; with questions of individual responsibility versus public responsibility; and with the role of the family as both heaven *and* hell. It is concerned with 'difficult' or 'risky' behaviours, and with the reasons for these behaviours. It is concerned with the ways in which inequalities and oppressions impact upon the psyches and the relationships of human beings and the cumulative impact of these. It is, in C. Wright Mills' famous phrase, concerned with 'public issues' and private troubles' and the relationship between them (Mills, 1959/2000). Given the essentially contested nature of its subject matter, for this reason, if for no other, it would be strange if social work itself did not reflect the contested nature of issues.

Guilt by Association

Since its beginnings in the late nineteenth century, social work has had the particular societal mandate of going amongst the poor, and working with the poor, but with the clear injunction 'not to go native' (the analogy with Christian missionary work in the remotest parts of the Empire is, of course, exact and early social work was often seen explicitly in these terms: Stedman-Jones, 1984). Jones refers to the ever-present danger of social workers becoming 'over-involved' with their clients as the problem of 'contamination' and sees the development of social work education as being part of a strategy to arm budding social workers against this danger (Jones, 1983). The dilemma this involved was evident from the earliest days of the Charity Organisation Society (COS). The Society's philosophy, *COS* which finds many echoes in the current moral authoritarianism of New Labour, will be discussed in Chapter 3, but it is worth noting here that even the strong, free-market ideology of the COS could sometimes be challenged by the contact of COS volunteers like Beatrice Webb with the realities of poverty:

> it was difficult to see how such [COS] principles could be 'made consistent with the duty persistently inculcated of personal friendship with the poor'. (Lewis, 1995: 56)

That threat became most pronounced during the 1970s with the advent of radical social work, when many social workers explicitly rejected the dominant explanations of the roots of their clients' problems in favour of structural explanations which led them to seek ways of engaging in joint action with clients against the policies of local and central government. However, even during periods when social workers have been much less politically involved, the simple act of 'friendship' with service users who are being demonised by government or the tabloid press, such as asylum seekers or young people in poor areas, can be seen as evidence of 'soft-headedness' or more recently, 'political correctness'. For many social workers, such guilt by association may be seen as 'coming with the territory', as the price to be paid for working in an ethical manner which only demonstrates respect for clients. In an article on political correctness and social work, Douglas cites the case of Alison, a social worker with Barnet Social Services, who

> 'sees the lack of resources as more relevant than ideology' .... . She sees no evidence of political correctness in her workplace. In her view, social workers have a responsibility to defend the rights of groups like asylum seekers who are treated poorly and with considerable prejudice at times by other professionals like benefits agency staff. If social workers are politically correct, that is fine if it helps to mitigate hostility to vulnerable groups. (Douglas, 1999: 46)

Troublesome Values

As the comments from Alison suggest, a further source of social work's awkwardness lies in its value base. This applies most obviously to the more radical social work values developed through the 1970s and 1980s, which became the basis of anti-oppressive practice (Shardlow, 1989; Braye and Preston-Shoot, 1994) but increasingly, it also includes more traditional social work values, such as respect for persons. As the demonisation and scapegoating of particular social groups, such as young people and asylum seekers, have continued and even intensified under New Labour governments (Butler and Drakeford, 2001), even these traditional values can begin to take on a radical edge and can force social workers to begin to challenge existing policies and practices. That 'being treated like a human being' was the thing homeless people valued most about the services they received was a key finding of research into homelessness and mental distress in Glasgow (Ferguson et al., 2005; more generally on the importance of respect, see Sennet, 2003). Conversely, the implications for mental and physical health of *not* feeling respected is evident in the following comment from an Afghani asylum seeker 'dispersed' to one of the most deprived areas of Glasgow:

> When people look down on you, when they don't respect you as a human being, then you feel very belittled. We think that people don't respect us like human beings. We have a responsibility to be part of the society but if people don't want us to be part of society, then we feel very segregated, very isolated. That affects us psychologically and mentally because we feel that nobody needs us, they don't respect us like any other human being. (Quoted in Ferguson and Barclay, 2002) .

Another traditional social work value which finds itself increasingly at odds with dominant ideas is a belief in people's capacity to change. Several writers have noted the shift in social policy over the past two decades from a discourse of rehabilitation, which emphasised people's capacity to change, to a discourse of risk management which emphasises risk minimisation and control (Parsloe, 1999; Webb, 2006). That discourse is now dominant within a number of areas, including mental health (particularly in relation to people with the diagnosis of personality disorder) as well as criminal justice (particularly in relation to sex offenders).

Emphasis on the Social

In contrast to theories of society which locate the roots of social problems *within* the individual, most social work theories, including most mainstream theories, have tended to emphasise the interaction *between* the individual and society (or 'environment'). To that extent social work challenges explanations of social problems which seek to reduce them to the behaviours of individuals. It is this emphasis on the 'social' which on the one hand permits a holistic approach to the understanding and response to people's problems and on the other, which has allowed social work, to a greater extent than any other profession, to contribute to the development of social models of disability and mental health over the past two decades (Oliver, 1996; Tew, 2005).

Making Sense

Gee, Officer Krupke, we're very upset;
We never had the love that ev'ry child oughta get.
We ain't no delinquents, We're misunderstood.
Deep down inside us there is good!

(*West Side Story*, Sondheim, 1957)

Sondheim's witty parody on the perceived tendency of social workers to seek to explain every form of human behaviour, no matter how dreadful or anti-social, has been mirrored in recent years in a much less amusing discourse which eschews such explanations in favour of a harsh moralism which seeks primarily to blame and punish. Its founding credo might well be the (then) Conservative Prime Minister John Major's response to the death of the two-year-old child Jamie Bolger at the hands of two other children, when, in an interview with the *Mail on Sunday*, he suggested that society needs to 'understand a little less and condemn a little more' (*Mail on Sunday*, 21 February 1993). 'Understanding' in this case should, of course, have meant acknowledging not only the dreadful upbringings experienced by the two children who had killed Jamie but also the fact that the murder of children by other children is extremely rare and that the numbers have not risen in recent years (Ferguson, 1994). The way in which this shift from 'depth' explanations of social problems, in the sense of explanations which look for meanings, to 'surface' explanations whose primary aim is to manage and control (Howe, 1996) will be explored later in this book. What is true, however, is that since its inception, a central concern of social work has been to *make sense* of people's behaviour, and to explore the *meanings* of clients' lives and relationships (England, 1986; Preston-Shoot and Agass, 1990). This is not, of course, an inherently radical activity. In the early days of social work, the main purpose of 'making sense' of clients' behaviour was to determine eligibility for charitable relief; while at other times, the framework for making sense has been a narrow individualistic one which precluded a whole range of possible explanations which emphasised wider societal processes (Mayer and Timms, 1970). Nevertheless, the recognition by almost every current in social work (other than, perhaps, some behavioural schools) that looking at alternative explanations of behaviour, 'hypothesising', is an essential part of the process of social work assessment and intervention is a given within most mainstream social work approaches (Hughes, 1995; Milner and O'Byrne, 2001). It is for that reason that a broad, in-depth knowledge base, which since the 1970s has included sociology and social policy as well as developmental psychology, should continue to be a core part of social work education (Simpson and Price, 2007). Part of the current impatience with social work stems from a dominant discourse which would prefer not to try to make sense of 'difficult' behaviours (not least since this might raise wider questions about the society in which we live) and rely instead on 'common sense' to locate the blame within 'dangerous' individuals or 'risky' families.

Holistic Practice

The recognition, drawn in part from a sociological knowledge base, that the roots of service users' problems often lie not with the individual or the family but in oppressive social structures and disempowering social processes pointed to the need for holistic responses which address service users' problem at whichever level seems most appropriate, be it individual, group, community or structural. Despite their limitations, it was this recognition which gave the ecological or systems approaches that came to the fore in the 1970s whatever radical potential they possessed (Leonard, 1975).

Ironically, thirty years after that 1970s' critique of the dominance of social work practice by one method, psychosocial casework, like community work, has also been eclipsed by the domination since the early 1990s of another US import, care management (Schorr, 1992), as the preferred vehicle for the introduction of market forces into social work (Harris, 2003). Rediscovering and re-valuing the full range of social work methods which permit a genuinely holistic response would seem to be an essential task in reclaiming social work.

Conclusion

Not all of the features described above are unique to social work. Other professions espouse similar values, emphasise the importance of process and relationship, draw on a knowledge base or use similar approaches. Social work, however, is more than the sum of its parts. The combination of a value base of respect, empowerment and social justice; the emphasis on a relationship between worker and service user founded on trust and non-judgemental acceptance; a knowledge base which embraces both developmental psychology and also an understanding of social structures and social processes; and a repertoire of methods ranging from individual counselling to advocacy and community work; all these give social work a holistic perspective which makes it unique amongst the helping professions. That perspective is reflected in the definition of social work adopted by the International Federation of Social Workers in 2000:

> The social work profession promotes social change, problem solving in human relationships and the empowerment and liberation of people to enhance well-being. Utilising theories of human behaviour and social systems, social work intervenes at the points where people interact with their environments. Principles of human rights and social justice are fundamental to social work. (www.ifsw.org.com)

It is also that combination of elements which gives social work the potential to be an *awkward* profession, as well as a profession worth preserving. Like Jones, Powell also argues that

> Social work's capacity to survive depends upon its legitimacy as an authentic 'humanising voice' rather than simply a conservative profession conveniently wrapping itself in the rhetoric of the market. (Powell, 2001: 16)

Later in this book, I shall explore some of means by which social work might rediscover its humanity, as well as its radicalism. Before then, however, it is necessary to examine in more detail the philosophy, policies and practice of the ideology that has shaped the experience of most of the world's peoples for more than a decade, as well as having created the current crisis in social work: neo-liberalism.

2

Neo-liberal Britain

Introduction: 1973 – the Year the World Changed

Life on Mars was a popular BBC TV drama series first screened in early 2006. It featured a young police detective who, after being struck by a car, wakes up to find himself transported back more than thirty years to 1973. He makes his way to a local police station where his arrival as a new senior detective in a team characterised by sexism, racism and crude investigative techniques has been anticipated. Each week the series portrayed the young man's increasingly frantic efforts to make sense both of the time warp within which he found himself and also of the very different world of Britain in the early 1970s. *Life on Mars* attracted a huge following, not only due to its imaginative storylines but also because of its identification of the profound ways in which life in Britain has changed over these three decades. At the most superficial level, there are the changes in dress and style (gone, the flared trousers and mullet haircuts). Then there are changes in technology: no PCs, Internet or mobile phones. Most striking, however, are the changes in popular values and attitudes which the series portrayed. For this was the world before the Steven Lawrence enquiry in 1999 branded the Metropolitan Police as institutionally racist, a world in which overt sexist and racist attitudes were often the norm (and not only in police canteens) and a world where minorities in general were afforded precious little respect. In that sense, the series showed how far Britain as a society has come as a result of the struggles against discrimination and oppression over these years.

The year 1973 is significant, however, for another reason not touched on by the series. For this was the year which saw the end of the 'long boom', the period of unprecedented world economic growth which followed the Second World War (Armstrong et al., 1991). During the 1950s and 1960s, poverty in Britain and other Western capitalist societies did not go away but many people in the West did experience a real improvement in their living standards. In addition, the creation of a Welfare State in Britain in 1948 meant that, for the first time, working-class people could enjoy a degree of security in the face of illness and unemployment (Timmins, 1996).

Not for nothing did the left-wing Labour MP Aneurin Bevan call his collection of essays on the Welfare State *In Place of Fear* (Bevan, 1952). These were years in which working-class people could begin to dream of a better life for themselves and their children than their own parents could ever have envisaged. The world economic crisis of 1973, triggered by a sharp rise in oil prices that year but reflecting much deeper structural problems, changed all that (Harman, 1984). It had three main consequences.

First, it led to the return of mass unemployment. In virtually all Western countries, unemployment which had hovered around the 1 or 2 per cent level for most of the post-war period doubled and then doubled again at the end of the decade. In Britain, the figure passed 1 million in 1979, higher than it had been since the Great Depression of the 1930s (Keegan, 1984).

Second, the economic crisis led to attacks on the Welfare State. Social work spending, for example, which had risen by 15.8 per cent under a Conservative government between 1970 and 1974 grew by only 1.9 per cent under a Labour government between 1975 and 1979 (Langan, 1993). The Kilbrandon Report in Scotland (1965) and the Seebohm Report in England and Wales (1968) had laid the basis for a social work practice which was preventative, inclusive and which, in Scotland, required local authorities to actively promote social welfare (Hartnoll, 1998). As Langan notes, however, the introduction of targeting of services to particular client groups by the new Labour Government at the end of 1974 meant that

> Within six years of Seebohm the selective mentality of the old Poor Law had come to prevail over the universalist aspirations of the report's more radical proponents. (Langan, 1993: 54)

Under pressure from the International Monetary Fund, public spending in Britain was reduced by 9.5 per cent in real terms after allowing for inflation between 1976 and 1978, a higher cut than was ever achieved in the subsequent years of Conservative government and one which resulted in the closure of large numbers of schools and hospitals (Cliff and Gluckstein, 1988; Elliot, 1993).

Third, it brought to an end the political and economic consensus which had existed between the two main political parties for most of the 1950s and 1960s (usually referred to as 'Butskellism', after Rab Butler and Hugh Gaitskell, leading figures in their respective parties at that time). Central to that consensus had been the ideology of Keynesianism, based on the ideas of the economist John Maynard Keynes and in practice involving an acceptance of the key role of the State in the provision of welfare, in the management of essential industries and in the regulation of the economy. Now Keynesianism was to be replaced by monetarism, the prototype of present-day neo-liberalism. Significantly, monetarist policies were introduced not by Margaret Thatcher but by the Labour Government of 1974–79, with a key shift signalled in the Labour Prime Minister James Callaghan's speech to Labour Party Conference in 1976:

> We used to think you could spend your way out of a recession, and increase employment by cutting taxes and boosting government spending. I tell you in all candour that that option no longer exists, and that in so far as it ever did exist, it only worked on each occasion since the war by injecting a bigger dose of inflation into the economy, followed by a higher level of unemployment as the next step. (Quoted in Cliff and Gluckstein, 1988: 322–3)

In practice, this increasingly meant a return to the free-market ideologies which had been discarded during the Great Depression of the 1930s, albeit adapted to the increasingly globalised world of the 1980s and 1990s.

This chapter will explore the promise and the reality of neo-liberalism. For over the past two decades, its central credo, first mooted by Margaret Thatcher, that there is 'no alternative to the market' has become the common sense not only of the political Right but also of most social democratic parties around the world, albeit often dressed up in the rhetoric of the 'Third Way'. In the next two chapters (Chapters 3 and 4), I shall explore the ways in which neo-liberalism has reshaped social work, and in Chapter 8, the final chapter, the ways in which the growing resistance to neo-liberalism both inside and outside social work is creating the conditions for a different kind of social work, rooted in social justice. First though, the rationale for neo-liberalism as well as its key elements will be explored. Thereafter, the core promise of neo-liberalism – that all would benefit from the extension of market forces as a result of wealth 'trickling down' from the richest to the poorest – will be critically assessed through an examination of poverty, inequality and insecurity in Britain in the first decade of the twenty-first century.

Neo-liberalism: The Promise

Neo-liberalism is best understood as a political and economic strategy, adopted initially by governments in Chile, Britain, the USA and New Zealand but thereafter throughout most of the world, to address the crisis of profitability which was exposed by the oil crisis of 1973. Its overriding concern was with restoring the health of capitalist economies – in particular, through increasing profitability. Harvey defines neo-liberalism as being

> in the first instance a theory of political economic practices that proposes that human well-being can best be advanced by liberating individual entrepreneurial freedoms and skills within an institutional framework characterized by strong property rights, free markets, and free trade ... . Furthermore, if markets do not exist (in areas such as land, water, education, health care, social security

or environmental pollution) then they must be created, by state action if necessary. (2006: 2)

In practice, this has meant two things. On the one hand, it has involved the creation of new markets, whether through the privatisation of existing State-owned utilities (such as rail, gas and water) or through the setting up of new institutional arrangements which allow market forces access to areas from which they have previously been excluded (in the case of health and social care services in Britain, through the purchaser/provider split introduced by the NHS and Community Care Act in 1990 – Harris, 2003; Pollock, 2004). On the other hand, it has involved the removal (or weakening) of what are perceived as barriers to the free operation of market forces, whether in the form of 'unnecessary regulation', trade unions or professional interest groups, such as doctors and lawyers. This latter process has taken place through a combination of international agreements (such as the General Agreement on Trade and Services), employers' offensives (such as Ronald Reagan's attack on the air traffic controllers' union in the USA in 1981 or Margaret Thatcher's war with British miners in 1984/85) or through an aggressive consumerism which employs notions of 'choice' and 'user empowerment' to undermine professional power.

Pratt identifies the three key elements of neo-liberal ideology as being first, *methodological individualism,* the notion that society is reducible to individuals pursuing their own self interests, so that, in Margaret Thatcher's famous phrase, 'there is no such thing as society, only individuals and families'; second, *rationality,* in the sense that individuals normally act rationally in pursuit of their own self-interest; and third, *market supremacy,* the belief that the market unhindered by impediments such as trade unions is the most rational way to organise society (Pratt, 2005: 12–13). Linked to this third element is the notion that everyone benefits from market society, in that while some people will grow much richer than others, wealth will also 'trickle down' to the poorer sections of the community (or in another much overused metaphor, 'in a rising tide, all boats rise').

All three of these elements are relevant to a discussion of the ways in which neo-liberalism has shaped welfare services and the experience of those who use them. The extreme individualism which Thatcher celebrated, for example, has over two decades contributed to what Lorenz has described as 'neo-liberalism's erosion of solidarity' (Lorenz, 2005a), a profound atomisation of social life vividly explored in movies such as Paul Haggis's *Crash,* and the consequences of which in the US context were all too evident to the poor black population of New Orleans following the devastation wrought by Hurricane Katrina in 2005. The notion that individuals always act rationally in pursuit of their own self-interest has underpinned the reconstruction of clients or service users as customers within a social care marketplace. However, it is primarily the third claim – the notion that neo-liberal policies benefit not just the rich but all members of society – that this chapter will seek to assess, focusing mainly on the experience of Britain under New Labour since 1997.

Neo-liberalism: The Record

What, then, has been the impact of the neo-liberal policies initiated by Conservative governments in the 1980s and continued under New Labour since 1997? Answering that question will involve us in looking at three distinct but related areas: poverty; inequality and insecurity.

Poverty

Hills and Stewart summarise the State of Britain when the first New Labour government took office as follows:

> The Labour Government that took office in 1997 inherited levels of poverty and inequality unprecedented in post-war history. More than one in four UK children lived in relative poverty, compared to one in eight when Labour had left office in 1979 .... . Poverty among pensioners stood at 21%. Income inequality had widened sharply: in 1979 the post-tax income of the top tenth of the income distribution was about five times that of the bottom tenth; by the mid-1990s that rate had doubled. (Hills and Stewart, 2005: 1)

Even these figures, however, fail to give a true picture of the huge redistribution of wealth – from poor to rich – which took place during these years, the spirit of which is best captured in novels such as Jonathon Coe's *What a Carve-Up!*. The Sunday Times 'rich list' in 1999, for example, showed that the wealthiest 200 people were worth £38 billion in 1989 but £75.9 billion in 1999 (Labour Research, 2000). In fact, during the 18 years of Conservative rule, the poor became poorer by £520 per annum while the incomes of the rich rose by more than £12,000 per year (Gordon, 2000: 34).

The issue of poverty is of considerable relevance to social workers for the simple reason that most people who use social work services are poor. As an American observer of British social work commented in the early 1990s:

> the most striking characteristics that clients of social services have in common are poverty and deprivation. Often this is not mentioned ... still, everyone in the business knows it. (Schorr, 1992: 8)

In 1997, Becker found that nine out of ten social work clients in the UK were in receipt of welfare benefits (Becker, 1997) while earlier in the decade Brandon had observed that 'the most common symptom of mental illness is poverty' (1991). The fact that 15 years later, 40 per cent of those claiming Incapacity Benefit were suffering from mental health problems suggests that little has changed (*The Guardian*, 26 January, 2006).

So how have poor people fared under New Labour? The incoming government's strategy in relation to poverty (and wealth) is explained in the following way by its most prominent academic supporter:

New Labour since 1997 has focused firmly on the poor. The reasoning is that the priority should be to concentrate on the most disadvantaged, rather than worry about overall levels of income inequality. The rich were to be largely left alone; it was far more important to concentrate on raising the floor – improving the economic and social position of the poor both in absolute terms and relative to median income. New Labour sought to break away from the traditional theme of the left that the rich must have become so by exploiting others. Those who are economically successful often bring benefits to wider society as a condition of their drive, initiative and creativity. (Diamond and Giddens, 2005: 103)

Leaving the rich alone meant that the traditional social democratic strategy for addressing poverty – wealth redistribution – was not an option. Rather, for New Labour, the road out of poverty lay through what Adler has called the 'employment model': getting people into paid work and subsidising low-paid employment through tax credits (Adler, quoted in Grover, 2006). As Jordan has argued, this emphasis on work has shaped every aspect of New Labour's welfare strategy, including its narrow understanding of social exclusion (as meaning primarily exclusion from paid work), the authoritarianism underpinning its welfare policies (since those reluctant to work, for whatever reason, must be 'helped' to do so, through policies such as the New Deal for the long-term unemployed) and the exclusion of social work from its welfare initiatives (since it is not seen as suited to the tough economic role these policies demand) (Jordan with Jordan, 2000).

How successful, then, has welfare-to-work been as a strategy for reducing poverty? A number of major studies have painted a comprehensive picture of poverty in Britain just under a decade after New Labour first came into office (Hills and Stewart, 2005; Palmer et al., 2005; Pantazis et al., 2006).

Thus in 2003/4, 12 million people in Britain – about one in five – were living in income poverty. This is nearly 2 million less than in the early 1990s. It is still, however, nearly twice what it was when the Conservatives came into office in 1979. In fact, since New Labour was elected, poverty levels have declined only amongst two groups: families with children (down from 32 to 29 per cent) and pensioners (down from 27 to 22 per cent). In contrast, the proportion of working-age adults without dependent children in income, poverty has actually increased by 400,000 since the late 1990s (Palmer et al., 2005).

Poverty has also grown amongst working-age disabled people, 30 per cent of whom live in income poverty as compared to 27 per cent a decade ago (Palmer et al., 2005: 13).

It is in relation to child poverty, however, one of only two areas where New Labour set themselves targets for reducing poverty, that the limitations of the current strategy are most obvious. At a lecture in 1999 in memory of William Beveridge, Tony Blair committed the government not just to reducing child poverty but to its abolition:

> Our historic aim [will be] that ours is the first generation to end child poverty forever.... It is a 20-year mission, but I believe it can be done. (Quoted in Hills and Stewart, 2005: 11)

The first stage in that twenty-year mission was to be a 25 per cent reduction – 1 million – in the number of children living in poverty by 2004/5. There was general agreement that this would be the easiest target for the government to reach, given that they would be moving those nearest to the poverty line over that line. Despite this, when the figures were announced in March 2005, they showed that the government was 30 per cent (or 300,000 children) short of its target. This meant that in 2006, 3.4 million children in Britain were still living in poverty. The conclusion drawn even by some sympathetic to New Labour was that, while progress had been made, a strategy of relying mainly on tax credits and a very low Minimum Wage would be insufficient to raise millions of children out of poverty and that substantial redistribution of wealth was required (Toynbee, 2006a). Others were much harsher in their criticism of the government's performance. Save the Children UK, for example, issued a press statement headed 'Blair Betrays' Britain's Children' and demanded an urgent enquiry into the failure to meet the target of 1 million (Save the Children, 2006).

In other areas too, there seems to have been little or no change. Thus, for example, the 50 per cent of children who qualify for free school meals – one of the most commonly accepted indicators of child poverty – still come from 20 per cent of schools, a figure unchanged since 1996 (Palmer et al., 2005: 33).

Moreover, while some commentators attribute the decline in child poverty that has taken place mainly to the impact of government policies, notably Working Families Tax Credits, this is not a universally shared view. Thus according to the authors of the Joseph Rowntree Poverty and Social Exclusion Annual Monitoring Report:

> It is the increase in employment rather than the increase in benefits which is primarily responsible for the fall in child poverty ... in-work benefits too, in the shape of tax credits, have played a limited direct role in lifting households out of poverty. (Palmer et al., 2005: 11)

While this may initially seem to lend support to the government's strategy of emphasising work as a way out of poverty, again this is not a conclusion drawn by most of these studies. Thus according to the Joseph Rowntree

Foundation's (JRF) study, 50 per cent of children in poverty are living in households where someone is doing paid work, most of them in two-adult rather than one-adult households. They go on to argue that

> However strongly employment grows in the future, there is no reason to believe that job growth alone will be able to reduce child poverty by 1.4 million between 2003/4 and 2010 when it has only managed to reduce it by 600,000 since 1998/9. (Palmer et al., 2005: 12)

The reason given by the authors is simple: low pay. The conclusion that 'work isn't working' is also drawn by the authors of the most comprehensive study to date of deprivation in Britain, the Poverty and Social Exclusion Survey (PSE).

> Many of those in paid work do not earn enough to lift them out of poverty. In-work benefits may supplement income but do not address the social exclusion that results from pressure on time, especially for those with caring responsibilities. Encouraging people to work longer hours is clearly not the answer to the problems of poverty and social exclusion. (Pantazis et al., 2006: 467)

Not surprisingly then, attacking low pay, including a substantial increase in the Minimum Wage, is seen by most of these authors as one of the more effective ways of challenging poverty.

There is however, a further difficulty with a strategy which places so much emphasis on paid work as the way out of poverty. As Hills and Stewart note:

> The improvements we describe in many areas have taken place while the economy has been growing steadily and indeed has been doing so for ten years. (Hills and Stewart, 2005: 345)

While on the one hand that means it may be harder to reduce relative poverty rates, it also suggests that it is an expanding economy (linked to the motor of the US economy) rather than solely specific government policies which is making the difference to poverty rates. If, however, that economy falters and unemployment begins to rise again, as it started to do in 2006, then even those small gains that have been made can be quickly wiped out. As former welfare minister Frank Field commented when the child poverty figures were announced:

> A major rethink of the government's anti-poverty strategy is now required, with unemployment rising, no new money to make a substantial lifer in the value of tax credits, and with the pot of money for major new welfare reform projects now empty. (Quoted in *Herald*, 10 March 2006)

In fact, only one year later, official figures showed that relative poverty in the UK had risen to 12.7 million in 2005–06 from 12.1 million the year before. More damningly, for a New Labour government which had made the eradication of child poverty a policy target, the number of children living in poverty also rose during that year from 200,000 to 3.8 million (*The Guardian*, 28 March 2007).

Finally it is necessary to set the government's poverty programmes in a wider political context. Whatever the limitations of a strategy that has combined an emphasis on work as the route out of poverty with targeted benefits, the fact that by 2006, 700,000 children had been lifted over the poverty line is to be welcomed and shows that government intervention and increased resources can make a difference. One can only wonder, however, how many more children might also have been lifted out of poverty by 2006 if only a small percentage of the £5.3 billion set aside to fund the ongoing war and occupation of Iraq had been targeted instead towards the ending of child poverty (*The Independent*, 13 March 2007).

Inequality: Does It Matter?

Reducing poverty, particularly child poverty and pensioner poverty, has been an explicit New Labour objective since the late 1990s. As the quote given above from Diamond and Giddens indicated, however, the same cannot be said of inequality. The flavour of government thinking in relation to inequality was famously conveyed by Tony Blair in an interview for the *Newsnight* programme:

> The issue isn't in fact whether the very richest person ends up becoming richer. The issue is whether the poorest person is given the chance that they don't otherwise have … the justice for me is concentrated on lifting incomes of those that don't have a decent income. It's not a burning ambition of mine to make sure that David Beckham earns less money. (Quoted in Sefton and Sutherland, 2005: 233)

The theoretical rationale for this view of inequality, which involves a significant break with traditional social-democratic approaches, is spelled out in more detail by David Goodhart, editor of the monthly journal *Prospect*:

> The old fixation with the gap [between rich and poor] is the problem. A third way theory of fairness should state that the gap does not matter – or at least that it matters less than the life chances of the people at the bottom. If these are rising steadily, then it does not matter that the rich are getting richer … . (Quoted in Callinicos, 2000: 14)

Unsurprisingly then, the trend towards inequality in Britain that began under the Conservatives has continued and intensified under New Labour. In his book *Rich Britain*, Lansley found that

> Britain has been slowly moving back in time – to levels of income inequality that prevailed more than half a century ago and to levels of wealth inequality of more than thirty years ago. (Lansley, 2006: 29)

According to a report published in 2004 by the Office for National Statistics, the wealth of the super-rich has doubled since Tony Blair came to power. Nearly 600,000 individuals in the top 1 per cent of the UK wealth league owned assets worth £355 billion in 1996, the last full year of Conservative rule. By 2002 that had increased to £797 billion. Part of the gain was due to rising national prosperity, but the top 1 per cent also increased their share of national wealth from 20 to 23 per cent in the first six years of the Labour government. Meanwhile the wealth of the poorest 50 per cent of the population shrank from 10 per cent in 1986 towards the end of the Thatcher government's second term to 7 per cent in 1996 and 5 per cent in 2002. On average, each individual in the top 1 per cent was £737,000 better off than just before Mr Blair arrived in Downing Street (ONS, 2004).

Some flavour of the 'greed is good' mentality that continues to flourish amongst the very rich in Britain and elsewhere was captured in a report in the *Independent* newspaper in early 2006. Headed 'Boom and Bust Britain', the article reported a study by leading thinktank the Centre for Economic and Business Research which showed that City traders were set to share a staggering £7.5 billion bonus pool after a bumper year for share prices and company takeovers:

> At the top end, about 3,000 people, usually at boardroom level at such companies as Goldman Sachs and Morgan Stanley, will get bonuses of more than £1m, with a handful nudging £10m .... . But there are also 330,000 City workers, usually traders, brokers and dealers, who are also getting bonuses, ranging from a few hundred pounds up to the magic £1m figure: the average is around £23,000. (Thornton and Kirby, 2006)

According to the article, sales of penthouses, luxury cars and champagne were at an all-time high. Meanwhile, however, a government report published the same week showed that more than 20,000 people were forced to file for bankruptcy in the three months running up to Christmas 2005 after being overwhelmed by their debts. The total of 20,461 was, apparently, a 51 per cent jump on the previous year and the highest number for a three-month period since records began in 1960. The total for 2005 was almost 70,000, 57 per cent higher than 2004. House repossessions, the article continued, were up by 70 per cent to the highest level since the 1991 crash.

In fact, contrary to the views of Third Way ideologues like Goodhart, inequality *does* matter, for three main reasons.

First, it matters on moral grounds. Most people intuitively see it as unacceptable that extreme poverty should coexist alongside such fantastic wealth. In early 2006, for example, the *Scotsman* newspaper carried a picture of two children born on the same day in different parts of Scotland. The life expectancy of the first child, born in an affluent village outside Edinburgh, was 87; the second child, born only 30 miles away but in one of the poorest districts of Glasgow, would be lucky to reach the age of 54 (*Scotsman*, 4 January, 2006). There is a link, in other words, between equality and notions of social justice (Powell, 2002). Within liberal political theory, the strongest case against such inequalities is contained in John Rawls' *A Theory of Justice* (Rawls, 1999). At the heart of Rawls' notion of 'justice as fairness' is the 'difference principle', the idea that inequalities can only be justified if they can be shown to work to the advantage of the least favoured groups in society. It is difficult to see what inequalities could justify a thirty-year difference in life expectancy.

Even amongst some prominent supporters of Third Way approaches there is growing disquiet about the impact of widening inequality and tentative calls for a 'new egalitarianism' (Giddens and Diamond, 2005). Such calls are based, first, on a Durkheimian concern with the consequences for community and social solidarity of blatant inequality and social divisions; second, with the implications of such inequalities for the self-respect of those at the bottom of the social heap. In respect of the first point for example, Ed Miliband has argued that

> It is increasingly clear in the modern age, for example in the literature on happiness, that higher consumption on its own does not provide fulfilment; a sense of citizenship and community is also important. And there are strong reasons for thinking it simply isn't possible to have a sense of community when vast inequalities of wealth and income mean that citizens are increasingly segregated in housing, schooling, etc. (Miliband, 2005: 45)

Miliband's point links to the second reason why economic inequality matters: namely its direct and indirect relationship with other forms of inequality. In relation to health inequalities, for example, on coming to office New Labour pledged to reduce the inequality gap by 10 per cent between 1997 and 2010. A study, however, by the Department of Health's own Scientific Reference Group on Health Inequalities in 2005 found the gap in life expectancy between the bottom fifth and the general population had actually widened by 2 per cent for men and 5 per cent for women between 1997–99 and 2001–03 (the first time, incidentally, this has ever happened under a Labour government). This means that life expectancy in the wealthiest areas is now 7–8 years longer on average than in the poorest areas (Department of Health, 2005).

Meanwhile the gap in the infant mortality rate between the poorest 10 per cent of people and the general population rose from 13 per cent higher in 1997–99 to 19 per cent higher in 2001–03. The infant mortality rate for the whole population was 5 deaths per 1,000 live births, compared to 6 per 1,000 among those with fathers in routine and manual work. This was significantly higher than the rate for those in the managerial and professional class, which was 3.5 per 1,000.

In one sense, none of this should surprise us. As studies from the Black Report in the late 1970s to the Acheson Report in the late 1990s have shown, there is a powerful correlation between class position and health (Whitehead et al., 1992; Acheson Report, 1998). In addition, the groundbreaking work of epidemiologist Richard Wilkinson strongly suggests that levels of inequality, rather than poverty alone, also contribute to this enormous waste of human life. Drawing on a vast amount of empirical data, Wilkinson concludes:

> Across the twenty five or thirty richest countries, there is no relationship between life expectancy and average income at purchasing power parities. Yet *within* each of these countries, health remains strongly related to income or any other socioeconomic marker. The paradox that health is related to income within the rich countries but not to income differences between them almost certainly arises because we are dealing with the health effects of *relative* income, social position or class. (Wilkinson, 2005: 184 – emphasis in original)

Such material inequality, moreover, is linked not only to health inequalities but also, as Wilkinson shows in his *The Impact of Inequality*, to levels of emotional health, violence and the quality of social relations between people, including levels of trust.

The third reason why inequality matters is that poverty is relational not only in the sense suggested by Wilkinson but in a further crucial sense. For contrary to what Goodhart argues in the passage quoted above, the US boom which has driven the world economy for the past two decades and swelled the personal fortunes of the individuals who run Microsoft, GAP, Shell and other corporations has been based primarily on quite unprecedented levels of exploitation of workers in America and elsewhere. In a discussion of the US economy, the respected Marxist economist Robert Brenner has argued that

> Between 1979 and 1990, real hourly compensation in the [US] private business economy grew at an average rate of 0.1 per cent. The trend in these years for hourly real wages and salaries (including benefits) was far worse, *falling* at an average rate of 1 per cent. At no time previously in the twentieth century had real wage growth been anywhere so low for so long. (Quoted in Callinicos, 2000: 10)

Similarly as the (non-Marxist) economic journalist Jeffrey Madrick comments:

> [T]he average real income of families was only a few percentage points higher in 1993 than in 1973, and that largely because so many more spouses were working. There have been shorter periods when wages have fallen sharply, but so far as we can tell, there has been no other twenty-year period since 1820 when average real wages fell, with the possible exception of the years just before and after the Civil War. (Quoted in Callinicos, 2000: 10)

The fact that the US boom is based on such hugely increased levels of exploitation, rather than the increased investment of the post-war boom, also means that its consequences – political, ideological and economic – are very different. As Harman comments:

> The contrast is all-important. The great post-war boom transformed the lives of tens of millions of US workers, making it seem that things would continually get

better under capitalism and that the American Dream could become a reality. The boom of the 1990s did not have anything like that effect. In fact it leaves one in eight Americans below the poverty line and nearly 45 million without health insurance. The fact that the top 5% of American families have seen a 64% increase in their incomes since 1979 does not in any way mitigate the way the bottom 60% have been running to stand still – with the bottom 20% going backwards. (Harman, 2001: 50)

Risk Society or Class Society?

Alongside persistent poverty and growing inequality, neo-liberalism has also created a society in which people feel much less secure, in which life seems much more precarious. The most influential theoretical exposition of this increased insecurity is provided by the German sociologist Ulrich Beck. In his *Risk Society*, Beck has argued that we have entered a new phase of modern society in which 'social, political, economic and individual risks increasingly tend to escape the institutions for monitoring and protection in society' (Beck and Ritter, 1992: 5). In this society, new risks or hazards emerge as by-products of the development of science, technology and industry. 'Mad cow disease' (BSE) or global warming would be two examples of such risks. However, whereas in earlier 'industrial society', risks were linked to class, poverty and inequality, now, Beck argues, *everyone* is at risk from the uncontrolled development of science and technology.

That there has been an increase in the level of risks that people experience in their daily lives is indisputable. It is also true that few, no matter how wealthy, can completely escape the effects of phenomena such as global warming. What is less convincing, however, is Beck's argument that risk (or the management of risk) has replaced accumulation as the dynamics of neo-liberal society, or that the risks that people experience and their capacity to respond to them are not shaped primarily by class divisions and inequality. In relation to the first point, Webb asserts that

In risk society political rule and power are less concerned with maintaining material provision and wealth than with regulation and compliance.... Arguably neoliberalism is *the* political programme of risk society. (2006: 38)

In fact, this is a topsy-turvy way of understanding what is going on. For as I have argued above, neo-liberalism is best understood as a *response* to a crisis of accumulation, a response based on the removal of all barriers to the incursion of market forces. If that response results in increased risk, whether environmental or social, then that is often a very secondary consideration for those whose primary concern continues to be with the accumulation of wealth. Global warming, for example, is not simply a product of the uncontrolled development of the forces of science and technology but rather stems from the insatiable desire of the oil and automobile industries for greater profits at any costs, whether human or environmental. It is the close links between these companies and national governments that explains the unwillingness of these governments, notably the US government, to sign up to agreements such as the Kyoto Agreement on Carbon Emissions which might, even in a small way, reduce the level of greenhouse gases. Second, while everyone is at greater risk, some continue to be at more risk than others. In relation to 'environmental' risks such as bird flu, for example, clearly those whose livelihoods are dependent on their livestock (including many millions of poor farmers in China and elsewhere) as well as those who have no choice but to eat cheap poultry (including many millions of people in the West) are considerably more at risk than those who have other sources of income or who can afford alternative types of meat. Third, an emphasis on environmental risk can lead to an underestimation of the social risks faced by those with limited financial resources in an increasingly privatised world. These might include the risk of being unable to find a decent school for your child when 'educational choice' increasingly means the capacity to move house to be near 'good' schools (Taylor, 2005); the risk of being unable to afford the costs of higher education and thus less able to compete effectively in a globalised marketplace; and, most worryingly of all for millions of people, the risk of being left without a decent pension in old age. As Levitas comments in a critique of Beck's thesis, in Britain:

> Genuine material need has increased with the rise in not just relative but absolute poverty since 1979, and the *removal* of welfare state protections (reduced eligibility for benefits, near collapse of the National Health Service, abolition of state provision for the elderly) and regulations (abolition of wages councils; refusal to accept the social chapter and working time directive). The sense of insecurity under these conditions derives from economic insecurity as well as environmental hazards. (Levitas, 2000: 205)

Compounding that sense of insecurity is the re-organisation of public services under New Labour around the concepts of 'choice' and 'personalisation' (to be explored more fully in Chapter 4) involving what Webb, following Rose, describes as the 'privatisation of risk' (Rose, 1999; Webb, 2006):

> The real issue of income inequality means that families and communities are afflicted with a huge burden of responsibility in having to sort out their own problems with a little push from the experts. Economic and structural disadvantage is ignored. (Webb, 2006: 62)

Conclusion

In this chapter, I have argued that the realities of neo-liberal policies in Britain as pursued first by Conservative governments and, since 1997, by New Labour have not lived up to the promise. While poverty levels may have been reduced for some groups, notably families with children, for others they have remained the same or worsened, despite a generally favourable economic situation. Even commentators sympathetic to the New Labour Project have argued that without much greater redistribution of wealth, in particular through taxing the rich, then it is highly unlikely that the government will come anywhere near achieving its stated objective of eliminating child poverty by 2020 (Toynbee, 2006b).

Then there is the belated recognition by New Labour strategists such as Anthony Giddens that inequality *does* in fact matter after all. Belated, since after almost a decade of New Labour government, the distribution of incomes was more unequal than at any time in recent history (Pantazis et al., 2006: 4). As we saw above, these income inequalities have been accompanied by growing health inequalities as well as falls in social mobility. Statistics alone, however, cannot convey the bitterness often felt by those at the bottom of the pile towards those who flaunt their ever-increasing wealth, or the sense of failure and lack of respect experienced by those who do not make enough money to 'count'. Some sense of what these many millions of people experience is provided by Sennett in his meditation on the meaning of respect:

> Lack of respect, though less aggressive than an outright insult, can take an equally wounding form. No insult is offered another person, but neither is recognition extended; he or she is not *seen* – as a full human being whose presence matters. When a society treats the mass of people in this way, singling out only a few for recognition, it creates a scarcity of respect, as though there were not enough of this precious substance to go round. Like many famines, this scarcity is man-made: unlike food, respect costs nothing. Why then should it be in short supply? (Sennett, 2003: 3)

Finally, neo-liberalism has led to a huge increase in insecurity in almost every area of life, including education, employment, health care, housing and pensions. Ironically, given New Labour's commitment to 'putting children first', this sense of insecurity is greatest amongst Britain's children. According to a UNICEF Report published in 2007 and based on an analysis of data from twenty-one economically advanced countries, children growing up in the UK suffer greater deprivation, worse relationships with their parents and are exposed to more risks from alcohol, drugs and unsafe sex than those in any other wealthy country in the world (UNICEF, 2007). They are, in the words of a *Times* newspaper commentary on the Report 'the unhappiest children in the Western World' (*The Times*, 14 February 2007). It would be hard to think of a more damning indictment of more than two decades of policies which, in Monbiot's phrase, have systematically put the interests of big business above those of society.

3

New Labour, New Social Work

Introduction

> Strangers embraced: 'Where were you when Portillo lost?' A seventy-year-old woman bought a rose for Tony Blair – 'If I live to be a hundred there'll never be another day like it!' ... In their wild euphoria they even talked of the night the Berlin Wall fell, of Nelson Mandela's release. It was the day the country exulted – even the sneering editorial writers at Wapping. (Toynbee and Walker, 2001: 1)

Toynbee and Walker's description of the scenes in Downing Street on the morning of 2 May 1997, following the defeat of the Conservatives in the previous day's General Election and Tony Blair's triumphant arrival at No. 10, captures well the mood throughout much of Britain on that day. After eighteen years of Conservative rule, many millions of people allowed themselves to believe that, in the words of New Labour's campaign song, things could, indeed, only get better. For many too in social work practice and education, the election of a Labour Government was a cause for hope and expectation. As we saw in Chapter 2, the previous two decades had witnessed a huge increase in the poverty and inequality experienced by many social work clients, even while the very use of the term 'poverty' was discouraged in government publications (Jones and Novak, 1999). Practitioners had grown increasingly demoralised as their competence and value base were repeatedly disparaged by ministers (including former social workers), who denounced them for 'political correctness' and called for their replacement by 'street-wise grannies' (Carvel, 2000). Meanwhile, against this background, social work, in all its aspects, was undergoing a profound reconstruction, with the welfarist project of Seebohm and Kilbrandon being abandoned in favour of a market-driven system with the central role allocated to care managers, required to focus primarily on budgets rather than client need (Parton, 1996).

In social work, as in many other areas of social policy, these early hopes and expectations were to be cruelly disappointed. As Orme and Jordan amongst others noted, New Labour's attitude to social work during its first term was characterised by uncertainty, ambivalence and mistrust (Jordan with Jordan, 2000; Orme, 2001):

> After two decades of Tory administration in which the future of social work had been uncertain, what was required was a clear commitment to a qualified social work and social care workforce to fulfil specific roles in the welfare system. However the most telling aspect of New Labour policy has been a lack of coherence. Despite the fact that many of the new politicians had a social work background, there was ambivalence in policies about welfare which brought little relief to those working in social work and social care and those involved in education and training. (Orme, 2001: 612)

In fact, the ambivalence to which these commentators refer concerned less the welfare policies which New Labour politicians wished to pursue than their confidence in the capacity of social workers to play a role in pursuing them: the extent to which, in other words, social work was (in a term often employed by a later New Labour Home Secretary) 'fit for purpose'. As we saw in Chapter 2, that purpose was enshrined in one policy which underpinned the whole project of welfare reform: work as the route out of welfare. As I shall argue below, that policy was also reflected in the two key themes of the 1998 White Paper for England and Wales, *Modernising Social Services*: First, there was the emphasis on *independence*, which stressed that 'those who can should live independently' while only those who could not should receive 'quality services' (Baldwin, 2002: 173). Second, the White Paper endorsed the shift introduced by the Conservatives in the early 1990s towards a market in social care and sought to move 'the focus away from who provides the care' and to place it instead on 'the quality of services' (Department of Health, 1998: 8).

While the aim, then, of New Labour welfare policy since that time – to create service user 'independence' within the context of a social care market – has been clear and consistent, two factors have contributed to doubt on the part of government about the capacity of the social work profession to contribute to this aim:

First, there is the issue of *competence*. There are two aspects to this. First, New Labour inherited from the Conservatives a view of social work as essentially a *failing* profession, a profession in need of reform. As Harris notes, within New Right theorising, social work was often presented as a metaphor for all that was perceived to be wrong with the Welfare State (Harris, 2003: 36). The evidence for this failure (other than perhaps the unspoken assumption that social workers should always be able to prevent the deaths of children at the hands of their carers) was seldom spelled out, but was asserted so often by politicians and the media over the past two decades that it gained the status of a self-evident truth. Second, there was the issue of whether social workers possessed the specific skills required by a welfare-to-work programme. Traditionally the focus of social work had not been the workplace, but rather the home and the community. It was perhaps predictable, therefore, that social workers would not be central to New Labour's reforms.

There was, however, another more important reason for New Labour's mistrust of the social work profession: namely, its value base, and the extent to which it could really be trusted to promote key New Labour policies in areas such as asylum, youth justice and 'welfare to work'. Butler and Drakeford, amongst others, have drawn attention to what they describe as New Labour's 'moral authoritarianism' (Butler and Drakeford, 2001). The ways in which that authoritarianism has clashed with core social work values, particularly in relation to notions of *dependence, independence* and *interdependence* will be explored below.

In practice, these concerns have led New Labour governments to adopt a twin-track strategy in relation to social work. On the one hand, as Jordan has argued, they have led to the exclusion of social workers from most of New Labour's key programmes, such as the New Deal programmes and Sure Start (Jordan with Jordan, 2000). On the other, they have sought to 'modernise' the social work profession in order to bring it into line with wider New Labour goals. Unsurprisingly, given the tensions between some of these wider goals and the ethical base of social work, a central element of that programme of modernisation has involved attempting to excise, or at least neutralise, that ethical base and to present social work as essentially a *technical* project, for example through an emphasis on (allegedly neutral) evidence-based practice (Gray and McDonald, 2006).

In the first section of this chapter, I shall explore the values and ideological assumptions which have underpinned New Labour welfare policy, and consider why they might cause problems for professional social work. The second section of the chapter will explore the ways in which New Labour have sought to 'modernise' social work and social care, and to harness them more closely to government goals and priorities. Harris has suggested that this project can best be understood in terms of three main interlocking themes: managerialism; the rhetoric of regulation; and consumerism (Harris, 2006). Here, I shall discuss the first two of these themes, while consumerism and its latest offspring, personalisation, will be discussed in Chapter 5.

New Labour, New Moralism

In a discussion of New Labour's welfare policies, Clarke has observed that

> New Labour emerged as a distinctly contradictory formation: committed to the modern, yet profoundly traditionalist; unevenly liberal and authoritarian; and both expansive and repressively containing. (Clarke, 2004: 132)

Nowhere is the traditionalist and authoritarian side of this apparent contradiction more evident than in New Labour's emphasis on morality and on the *active* remoralisation of the poor (Lavalette and Mooney, 1999; Jordan with Jordan, 2000). This emphasis on morality has not been confined to the field of welfare reform. By the third term of his administration, former prime minister, Tony Blair frequently justified many of his government's policies, including, for example, the invasion and occupation of Iraq, the dismantling of comprehensive education and the extension of market forces into the NHS by the simple assertion that 'it is the right thing to do.' It is, however, in New Labour's attitude towards poor people (and, importantly, to those who work with them) that this moralising emphasis is most explicit.

This class dimension of New Labour's approach to morality was noted by a *Guardian* leader in 1999 following a speech by Blair on the evils of teenage pregnancy:

> Blair has put 'moral' on the masthead [of government policy]. And for all his fine talk of modernising Britain it is clear his understanding of that loaded word is saloon-bar suburban: it means sex … [but his] moral does not … cover sex at large … Moral means to him what it did to Octavia Hill in the 1880s: the evils of poor people fornicating. (Quoted in Lavalette and Mooney, 1999)

While this is too narrow an interpretation of New Labour's approach to morality, the reference to Octavia Hill is, nevertheless, telling. There are indeed strong similarities between New Labour notions of what is moral, and the ideology and practices of the nineteenth-century Charity Organisation Society (COS) of which Hill was a founding member. Some flavour of the ethos of that organisation is provided by Whelan in his (sympathetic) history of the COS. He cites a case where a male breadwinner's failure to hold down a job resulted in the family going into the workhouse. The COS member involved commented:

> Would it not have been better in the beginning to have investigated why a skilled carpenter was always out of work, then to have refused charity, and simply to have urged the man to the moral effort, which would then have saved him? The charity given only encouraged him in his habits of sloth. (Quoted in Whelan, 2001)

While in the early twenty-first century, the language used to explain the de-moralisation of poor people may have changed, the core COS notion that the poor need to be coerced into behaving morally, often through the medium of a 'personal relationship' with a 'friendly visitor', is also at the heart of New Labour's welfare strategy (even if the 'friendly visitor' now comes in the form of a New Deal Personal Adviser). Jordan has described New Labour's mechanism for achieving such model citizens as 'tough love', a combination of carrot and stick, with the carrot being targeted benefits (aimed mainly at families with children), personal advisers and training opportunities, and the stick usually involving some combination of increased surveillance and the threat to cut benefits (Jordan with Jordan, 2000: 47). As Callinicos argues in his critique of the Third Way, however, far from such 'tough love' being in opposition to, or contradicting, New Labour's modernising economic agenda, in fact, the two approaches complement each other:

> There is ... an important sense in which New Labour authoritarianism is a consequence of Gordon Brown's version of neo-liberal economics ... if macro-economic stability is secured and the right supply-side measures are in place, any further unemployment is voluntary. Unemployment in these circumstances is a consequence of the dysfunctional behaviour of individuals who refuse to work, and this behaviour must in turn be caused either by their individual moral faults or by a more pervasive 'culture of poverty'. The kind of coercion implicit in the New Deal for the long-term unemployed, where government benefits are denied to those refusing to take part, is therefore legitimate. (Callinicos, 2001: 62)

The two key pillars of such 'tough love' are an emphasis on 'personal responsibility' on the one hand, and on a particular understanding of 'community' on the other. Each of these concepts will be considered in turn.

Independence and Personal Responsibility

Within New Labour ideology, where attempts to draw attention to the structural factors which shape people's lives are often portrayed as 'making excuses', the supreme principle is 'personal responsibility', the overriding strategy 'responsibilisation' (Young, 1999). The principle, of course, is hardly a new one; it was, as noted above in the COS example, a central pillar of Victorian morality. What is different or 'modern' about New Labour's spin on this essentially nineteenth-century worldview, however, is its economic content, as well as the context in which it is being deployed. For within the New Labour lexicon, personal responsibility primarily means equipping yourself with the skills to compete effectively in a globalised marketplace. That includes behaving prudently by putting aside money for your pension, mortgage or student loan, regardless of your income; maintaining your health and fitness by exercising, not smoking; and not becoming obese so that you do not become a 'drain' on State resources. Above all, it means striving to be 'independent', with the good citizen being the person who relies on his/her own resources and does not draw on the resources of the State. Here we see the overlap between morality, community and social exclusion. As Grover has noted:

> In its political use ... the idea of social exclusion has been reduced to concerns with exclusion from paid employment ... in a process that individualises exclusion

rather than taking seriously its embeddedness in social and economic practices. (Grover, 2006: 2)

Some of the consequences of this view of independence and personal responsibility are spelled out by David Harvey in his study of neo-liberalism:

It is precisely in such a context of diminished personal resources derived from the job market that the neoliberal determination to transfer all responsibility for well-being back to the individual has doubly deleterious effects. As the State withdraws from welfare provision and diminishes its role in arenas such as health care, public education and social services ... it leaves larger and larger segments of the population exposed to impoverishment. The social safety net is reduced to a bare minimum in favour of a system that emphasizes personal responsibility. Personal failure is generally attributed to personal failings, and the victim is all too often blamed. (2006: 76)

Given this context, the requirement to display personal responsibility falls more heavily on some sections of the population than on others. Specifically, as Bauman has noted, there often appears to be a yawning chasm between the expectations placed on poor people to take responsibility for their behaviour and the apparent unwillingness of those in positions of power and privilege to do so themselves (Bauman, 2005: 86). In part, that unwillingness to take responsibility is simply a case of old-fashioned hypocrisy and double standards, a case of 'do as we say, not as we do'. In part, however, it reflects the fact that while the 'irresponsible' behaviour of the poor is seen as a possible threat to the smooth running of the economy, such behaviour by those at the top is seen as relatively harmless. Similarly, the 'personal responsibility' discourse is rarely employed in relation to the practices of the wealthy middle classes – such as purchasing a second home, driving an SUV or relying on air travel when other forms of transport are available – despite the fact that all of these 'lifestyle choices' might well be seen as highly irresponsible, given their damaging effects on local communities, health and the environment.

Promoting the independence of service users and encouraging them to take personal responsibility for their own actions are, of course, bread and butter activities for many social workers and are closely linked to common-sense notions of empowerment. The way in which these notions are currently promoted by New Labour, however, carries two main dangers. First, welfare-to-work strategies which exhort people to become more independent, including government proposals in 2006 to reduce by up to a million the number of people claiming incapacity benefit, without properly addressing the factors, personal and structural, which limit their ability to do so are likely to be experienced (with justification) as punitive and could worsen people's physical or mental health (Ferguson, 2006). Second, as Lorenz has argued, social workers need to challenge narrow and potentially punitive notions of dependence and independence which simply do not fit the experience of many service user groups, including older people or those with severe impairments. Rather, as he argues:

Dependency and interdependency as such are not a threat to human endeavour, they are the necessary pre-conditions, but the structures and processes that establish networks of order and solidarity need to be negotiated rather than imposed. This is an experience that every social worker makes at the personal level with all types of users of social services, and this experience has a direct structural and political equivalent for which social workers are not only responsible, but are also uniquely equipped in terms of their skills and experience. What is necessary now is to bring these different levels of experience (which a controlling political agenda often wants to keep separate) and to work on different strategies jointly to overcome the fundamental threat of fragmentation, individualisation and the informalisation of social relations. (Lorenz, 2005a: 100)

Community

If personal responsibility is one key plank of New Labour's moral agenda, then the other is community, which Callinicos describes as the Third Way's 'all subsuming concept' (Callinicos, 2001). The Third Way's emphasis on community stems in part from the recognition of the divisive and fragmenting approach of unbridled market forces, in part from a concern (usually associated with political conservatism) about the implications of a perceived breakdown in community and family life (a concern also reflected in New Labour's emphasis on social inclusion – Pantazis et al., 2005).

In a newspaper article in the summer of 2004, then Prime Minister Tony Blair sought to locate the blame for this alleged decline in family, community, and law and order on the culture of the 'swinging sixties', a decade in which

A society of different lifestyles spawned a group of young people who were brought up without parental discipline, without proper role models and without any sense of responsibility to others. All of this was then multiplied in effect by the economic and social changes that altered the established pattern of community life in cities, towns and villages .... Today, people have had enough of this part of the 1960s consensus. People do not want a return to old prejudices and ugly discrimination. But they do want rules, order and proper behaviour. They want a community where the decent law-abiding majority are in charge. (*Evening Standard*, 19 July 2004)

There is no doubt that the ties binding many once-strong working-class communities have loosened over the past three decades. It is also true that the 'traditional' two-parent family unit is no longer the norm in the UK and that the number of families headed up by a lone parent, as well as the number of single-person households, has increased significantly during the same period. The reasons for these changes, however, are very different from those suggested here.

In part, they reflect the changing position of women in society. Women today are less willing than their mothers or grandmothers were to remain in abusive relationships and would often prefer to bring up a child on their own, despite the hardships that involves. Such a choice became available consequent on the huge social changes of the 1960s which, among other things, challenged traditional notions of women's roles, as well as the stigma of illegitimacy.

More important in the decline of community, however, than any lifestyle choices made by individuals was the profound damage, both material and spiritual, wreaked on working-class communities by the mass unemployment created by the policies of the Thatcher governments in the 1980s. In targeting the 1960s as the source of the breakdown of community, Tony Blair is focusing on the wrong decade. As Nick Davies concluded in his powerful study of poverty in Britain in the 1990s:

> Labour thinking seems to take no account of the damage which has been inflicted on the poor in the past twenty years. It assumes that even though these communities have been riddled with drugs and drink and depression and stress; that even though tens of thousands of young people have abandoned their schools without any thought for the future; even though hundreds of thousands are now unskilled and alienated while millions have been drained of hope and motivation; that nevertheless by flicking the switches of the benefits machine, these people can be manipulated into families or into work or out of crime as though they were carefully calculating their self-interest, as though their lives and sometimes their personalities had not been scrambled by the experience of the last twenty years. (Davies, 1998: 303)

If New Labour misdiagnoses the reasons for the collapse of so many working-class communities, then not surprisingly their prescriptions for 'strengthening' these communities are similarly misdirected. As several commentators have noted (Lavalette and Mooney, 1999; Butler and Drakeford, 2001; Grover, 2006), they are underpinned by a right-wing version of communitarian philosophy which sees community as first and foremost a mechanism of social control, and a vehicle for disciplining and regulating the behaviour of its more wayward members (Jordan with Jordan, 2000: 50). Perhaps not surprisingly given Tony Blair's distaste for the 1960s, insofar as there is a 'Golden Age' of community for New Labour it seems to be the 1950s, an era when young people seemingly did what they were told and when families stayed together no matter what. In fact, as we know from movies such as *Vera Drake* or *Pleasantville*, this was also the decade where the lives of many millions of women were cramped and suffocating, which saw the emergence of the 'juvenile delinquent' (as well as moral panics around 'Teddy boys' – Fyvel, 1961; Pearson, 1983), and where any form of diversity was frowned upon.

In its understanding of community, it is difficult not to be struck once again by the contrast between New Labour's unrelenting rhetoric of modernisation and the extremely conservative content of many its policies. As one commentator sympathetic to the New Labour project has noted:

> The communitarian critique of market capitalism is superficially appealing but eventually disappointing. Strong communities can be pockets of intolerance and prejudice. Settled, stable communities are the enemies of innovation, talent, creativity, diversity and experimentation. They are often hostile to outsiders, dissenters, young upstarts and immigrants. Community can too quickly become a rallying cry for nostalgia; that kind of community is the enemy of knowledge creation, which is the well-spring of economic growth. (Leadbetter, quoted in Callinicos, 2001: 66)

There may however be material as well as ideological and electoral reasons for this support for views which often seem to mirror the letters pages of the *Daily Mail* or the *Daily Telegraph*. A glimpse into the private lives of New Labour ministers was provided in early 2006 when it emerged that David Mills, husband of New Labour Minister Tessa Jowell had received a 'gift' of £350,000 from Italian Prime Minister Sergio Berlusconi which he had used to pay off a mortgage, without apparently telling his wife. Leaving aside the claims and counterclaims in the case, as one former British ambassador observed, the case highlighted the massive gulf between the fabulously wealthy lives of some New Labour ministers on the one hand and the many people in Britain who are struggling to make ends meet (Murray, 2006). Nor were the Jowell/Mills family an exception. The former prime minister Tony Blair's wife Cherie Blair, for example, bought two city centre flats in Bristol for £267,500 each and then in 2004 with her husband bought a house in Connaught Square in north-west London for £3.5 million (*Observer*, 2 April 2006). Against that background, exhortations from the dinner tables of New Labour ministers in Islington to poor people to take on greater 'personal responsibility' for their lives and finances can sometimes bear similarities to proclamations issued from the Courts of the Bourbons and Romanoff's, prior to the French and Russian Revolutions.

Modernising Social Work

If the remoralisation of 'dependent' individuals and communities is one key theme of New Labour ideology, then the other is modernisation. As noted above, the seeming contradiction between a conservative and often highly authoritarian emphasis on family and community on the one hand, and a ceaseless repetition of the importance of 'modernisation' and the 'modern' is more apparent than real. For like 'independence' and 'community', modernisation has a very specific meaning for New Labour. Above it all, it means bringing individuals, communities and institutions, whether professional or governmental, into line with the perceived requirements of a globalised world economy. And within social work, the chosen means to achieve such modernisation, were managerialism, regulation and consumerism. The first two will be discussed here, along with the notion of 'evidence-based practice', while consumerism will be discussed in Chapter 5.

Managerialism

The origins of what Clarke has described as the 'universalisation of management' (Clarke, 2004: 121), in the sense of more effective management being presented as the panacea for just about every problem facing public services, go back as far as the mid-1980s (Timmins, 1996). For the Conservative administrations of these years, public sector managers, reinvented in government discourse as dynamic individuals with vision, were the 'Bolsheviks' who would overthrow the bureaucratic and professional barriers to change and create a vibrant 'mixed economy of care' with a flourishing private sector (Langan and Clark, 1994). Appropriately enough then, the blueprint for the creation of such a social care market – the Griffiths Report of 1988, was provided by the director of Britain's leading supermarket chain. Over the next decade, one consequence of managerialism becoming the new common sense of public sector organisations was the widespread replacement of former professional social workers as senior managers by those with no professional social work qualification, a practice which has continued under New Labour. But the alleged benefits of this new conception of management were not to be confined to the upperlevels of public sector organisations. Drawing on US models (Schorr, 1992) and on the recommendations of the Griffiths Report, the 1990 NHS and Community Care Act and its associated guidance identified assessment and care management as *the* core social work roles, with the care manager as the individual who would assess need and co-ordinate 'packages of care' in a brave new world where 'purchasers' and 'providers' would no longer to be the same people or organisations. Veiled by a rhetoric of 'empowerment', 'choice' and 'needs-led assessment', the effect of these changes on traditional social work practice was to be profound. As Harris comments:

> The direction in which managerialism took social work after the establishment of the social work business was away from approaches that were therapeutic or which stressed the importance of casework, let alone anything more radical or progressive. Turning professionals into managers involved making them responsible for running the business. (Harris, 2003: 66)

Following the election of a New Labour government in 1997, that emphasis on the central role of management was retained, and even intensified, but given some new twists. Three distinctly New Labour additions can be identified.

New Labour
– managerialism intensified

First, whereas Conservative governments were generally happy to delegate power to managers and let them get on with it, in contrast, New Labour has tended to favour a 'franchise' model in which targets and standards are set centrally and then delegated to semi-independent bodies, such as the Social Care Institute for Excellence, to achieve, subject to a regime of tight regulation (Harris, 2003). The implications of this emphasis on regulation will be discussed in the next section.

Second, they have sought to promote identification with the organisation, rather than with a specific profession. As Clarke suggests, this involves the tendency

> To shift what were occupational/professional identities to ones that are organisation-centred. The organisation – the trust, the school, the department – seeks to become the point of identification, loyalty and commitment, with externally oriented provision being treated as suspect and as a 'special interest' that distracts from the 'organisation as common purpose'. (Clarke, 2004: 121)

Third, there has been an emphasis on the 'integration of services' as the key to more effective service delivery. In the words of an Audit Commission Report:

> Since 1997, the Government has stressed the need for organisations and government departments to co-operate more closely in the delivery of public services, placing the service user, or citizen, at the centre. This emphasis is reflected in the many multi-agency, cross-cutting structures which have emerged in the past few years, such as the various action zones, youth offending teams, drug action teams and the range of bodies addressing regeneration and urban renewal. (Audit Commission, 2002)

In practice, this has often involved the merger of previously independent social work departments with housing departments, education departments or health boards. There are obvious benefits in health, social work and other professions working together, in terms of breaking down cultural barriers, reducing duplication of services and leading to more effective sharing of information. There are also downsides to integration and partnership, however. In practice, the more powerful professions and agencies, such as health-based professions, are likely to dominate at the expense of the less well-organised or less prestigious professions and agencies, such as social work and voluntary sector organisations (Johnson et al., 2003). In addition, the loss of an organisational base, coupled with a weak professional identity, can lead to the virtual disappearance of professions such as social work, in the way predicted by Clarke some years previously (Clarke, 1996). Finally, even in cases where integration of services does appear to benefit service users (as, for example, in the integration of health and homeless services in Glasgow – Ferguson et al., 2005) this is often due to a high level of spending on pilot or specialist services which may not be maintained when these services go 'mainstream'.

The Rhetoric of Regulation

As noted above, if the Conservative governments of the 1990s were happy to place their faith in managers to bring about the required transformation in health and social work services, in contrast, New Labour's approach to professionals such as social workers has been much more interventionist. As Harris has argued, this has involved a highly centralist approach to policy-making, with responsibility for policy implementation 'franchised' to quasi-independent bodies which are in fact closely regulated and controlled from the centre (Harris, 2003: 84–6). Thus, new bodies such as the Social Care Council and the Social Care Institute for Excellence have been established in England and Wales to regulate (respectively) the workforce and social work's knowledge base, with equivalent bodies also set up in Scotland and Northern Ireland. Processes of external review, audit, inspection, national standards, as well as performance indicators covering almost every area of work, are now common features of social work and social care.

There are two distinct, if related, reasons for this increased emphasis on regulation and inspection: First, there is the mistrust of the professions, inherited from the Conservatives, with social work in particular often singled out as a failing profession. Greater regulation of the workforce is necessary because social workers cannot be trusted to bring about the necessary changes themselves. As noted earlier, precisely how social work is failing, or the reasons for that failure are seldom spelled out. That very lack of precision, however, can perform a useful political function. Consider, for example, one recent version of the 'social work is failing' theme, as delivered in the first 'message' of the 21st Century Social Work Review in Scotland, that 'Doing more of the same won't work'. The reason for this, apparently, is that

> The demand for social work services is increasing and changing as people's needs are becoming more complex and challenging. The expectations of citizens of the 21st Century are for more accessible, responsive public services of the highest quality. The result is that we expect more and more of a fixed resource, placing ever increasing pressure on social work services to deliver. Professional roles too often become focused on managing access to existing services rather than on helping people find solutions to their problems. In this way, people become passive recipients of services rather than active participants in their care. We have concluded that this is an unsustainable direction for social work services and that simply pouring more money into a service based on welfare models rather than the promotion of individual wellbeing, will not, in itself achieve a sustainable future. (Scottish Executive, 2006a: 10)

Much of this passage is empty rhetoric but it does merit some deconstruction, since its unquestioning acceptance of several key New Labour assumptions neatly illustrates the way in which the 'social work is failing' discourse can usefully underpin and justify greater regulation. First, there is the silence on context. People's needs may indeed be becoming 'more challenging and complex' but with life expectancy in some parts of Scotland as low as fifty-four, basic needs are likely to continue to figure highly on any social work agenda. Second, no evidence is provided for the assertion that it is 'increased expectations' on the part of service users that is placing ever-increasing pressure on this 'fixed resource' of social work services (and why does it have to be a 'fixed resource'?). Third, there is the familiar theme of 'active citizen' versus 'welfare dependent', with no acknowledgement that dependency on the part of some service users (older people with dementia, for example) is both normal and appropriate. And finally, there is the acceptance of the key managerialist assumption that 'pouring more money' into the service is unlikely to bring about any improvement, despite evidence to the contrary.

Contrast this view of why social work is failing with the views of an experienced social worker in an English local authority interviewed by Jones as part of his research into frontline social work:

> Social work is more and more about numbers, with managers wanting to hit so many targets which involves turning cases over quickly. They want a case in, sorted and pushed out. We have many unallocated cases so there is great pressure on everyone to take the maximum number of cases, to make it seem we are giving a service to the public. But we don't give anything. We have nothing to give. (Jones, 2004: 100–1)

In this example, the 'failure' of social work is seen as intimately bound up with the imposition of a quasi-business regime which subordinates the needs of service users and the skills of social workers to the demands of financial competition within a social care market. Nowhere in *Changing Lives*, in contrast, is there any analysis of the way in which the whole-sale introduction of care management approaches, as a core element of the wider marketisation of social work and social care, is contributing to the 'failure of social work'. Unsurprisingly then, given this analysis, the response of the Scottish Executive to the Report is to prescribe precisely more of the same managerialist formula which the social workers in Jones' study identify as contributing to the problems in the first place.

The second reason for the increased emphasis on regulation under New Labour is also associated with mistrust, but of a different kind. It stems from the Third Way concession to traditional social democratic thought that while markets and competition in social care as elsewhere offer the best guarantee of choice and high quality services, nevertheless a degree of regulation is necessary to ensure that they are functioning efficiently and to ensure that standards are maintained. Best Value frameworks, national standards, audits, league tables and inspection are some of the main ways in which what Webb has described as a 'performance man-agement and audit culture' is created (Webb, 2006). Despite the emphasis on 'continuous improvement', however, there is little evidence that such regimes of regulation, based on 'naming and shaming', do actually lead to better quality services. Rather, as Harris argues, and as the social workers quoted earlier suggest, they lead to organisations adapting to meet their performance targets, even though that means a poorer service for clients:

> As audit is associated with dysfunctions and pathologies it 'shrinks trust' (Power, 1997), with a constant flow of naming and shaming reports and stories about untrustworthy services appearing and indicating the need for more audit. Assumptions of distrust become self-fulfilling as audiences adapt their behaviour to the audit process, distorting reality so that it conforms to an auditable reality and becoming less trustworthy as a result of a process designed to make them more trustworthy. (Harris, 2003: 94–5)

Webb notes two other consequences of this 'performance culture' (Webb, 2006: 184–6). First, the social work role is increasingly conceived in terms of low-level assessment and planning. 'Joint working' means the use of assessment tools (such as Single Shared Assessment) that 'anyone can do' and hence, contributes to the process of deprofessionalisation.

Second, it changes the relationships between care managers, frontline workers and service users, with the role of care managers increasingly focused on the management of budgets and the reduction of risk. To quote a worker from the study by Jones cited above:

> Being a care manager is very different from being a social worker as I'd always thought of it. Care management is all about budgets and paperwork and the financial implications for the authority, whereas social work is about people. That's the difference. (Jones, 2004: 100)

Evidence-based Practice

The final aspect of the modernisation of social work to be considered here concerns its knowledge base. As with other areas of health and social care, modernisation in this context is understood to mean primarily the development of a social work practice based on verifiable research evidence. It is the use of such evidence, it is suggested, that will provide the best guarantee of the *effectiveness* of practice, which is, at the end of the day, the only consideration that really matters: 'what counts is what works.' In that sense, evidence-based practice (EBP) appears to be ideologically neutral, since the source of the evidence is unimportant, only its effectiveness for practice.

To implement this model of practice in the UK, New Labour has created several new bodies, including the Social Care Institute for Excellence (SCIE) in England and Wales and, north of the border, the Scottish Institute for Excellence in Social Work Education (SIESWE), loosely based on the model of the National Institute for Clinical Excellence which promotes EBP in the field of medicine.

As with other New Labour keywords (Williams, 1975; Ferguson, 2007), such as 'choice' or 'personalisation', it seems hard, even contrary, to be *against* the concept of evidence-based practice, and in fact, some of its proponents have suggested that it is unethical to be so, since service users should experience only intervention which have been shown to be 'effective', on the basis of good research (Sheldon, 2001). Yet despite this, EBP has been subjected to powerful criticism from a range of writers, usually from within the critical social work tradition (to be considered in Chapter 7). The objections fall into three main categories: the meaning of evidence; the nature of social work; and the political context in which EBP is being promoted.

The meaning of evidence. Earlier in this chapter, we noted the apparent contradiction that a government whose overriding commitment is to the 'modern' and the 'modernisation' should nevertheless embrace highly traditional and conservative understandings of community, family and other such concepts. Similarly, in the field of EBP, understandings of what constitutes evidence seem to rely heavily on narrow and highly traditional positivist conceptions of science, with two methods in particular – randomised control trials and meta-analyses – seen as superior to all other sources (Glasby and Beresford, 2006). Three objections have been made to this reliance on these methods (Cohen et al., 2004, quoted in Glasby and Beresford, 2006: 270). First, they have not been shown to be more reliable than other approaches; second, they can answer only limited questions; third, they do not include other non-statistical forms of knowledge. In respect of the second point, the fact that the outcomes of some approaches (such as cognitive-behaviour therapy) are more easily measurable than others (such as person-centred or psychosocial approaches) does not mean they are necessarily more effective, especially in the longer term (For a critique of the increasing reliance on cognitive behavioural approaches with in government mental health policies, see Holmes, 2002). In relation to the third point, in practice the prioritisation of these methods can lead to the neglect of other forms of evidence which may be more or equally valid and useful for social workers including, for example, service user accounts or epidemiological evidence on health inequalities which does not fit neatly into a narrow 'What Works' framework (Pilgrim and Rogers, 2002). In Chapter 8, we shall discuss the ways in which the neglect of such forms of evidence in semi-official policy documents may lead to the implementation of mental policies which could be potentially harmful to users of mental health services.

The nature of social work. Among the factors driving evidence-based approaches is the desire to reduce risk and increase certainty in social work. The Report of the 21st Century Review of Social Work in Scotland, for example, is explicit in making the link between greater use of research evidence and the reduction of risk.

f

> Because of this [i.e. the weakness of the evidence base for practice – IF], there is a need for a national research and development strategy for social work services, which not only develops new evidence but presents existing evidence in a way which informs practice and develops the expertise in the workforce to use and evaluate its impact. *An immediate priority within this strategy should be the development of nationally agreed risk assessment tools that provide a sound underpinning for professional judgement.* (Scottish Executive, 2006a: 55 – my emphasis)

The reduction of harmful risk to vulnerable service users, whether children or adults, is, of course, a goal which all would support. However, as many commentators have noted (e.g. Parton, 1996; Watson and West, 2006; Webb, 2006), while an emphasis on risk assessment frameworks may provide the illusion of being 'objective' and scientific, in reality their capacity to predict risk is limited, especially when the risks in a particular situation are considered in isolation from client's need.

More generally, there are problems with the rather mechanical way in which it is assumed social workers will 'apply' knowledge or empirical research evidence to practice. In this respect, as Gray and McDonald note:

> The adoption of evidence-based practice can best be understood as a continuation of long-standing attempts to deal with the ubiquity of ambiguity and uncertainty in social work. (2006: 12)

Yet as they and others argue, uncertainty and contingency are at the core of social work practice. The idea that these factors can be eliminated by the 'appliance of science' rests on a false view both of social work and also of how practitioners use knowledge to make sense of people's lives and situations.

The political context. As Gray and McDonald rightly argue, evidence-based practice is intensely political in intent (2006: 17). For if social work is to be made fit for the purposes which New Labour envisages, then its needs to be stripped of those aspects which, as we saw in Chapter 1, make it an awkward or troublesome profession; above all its value base. In the same way as the avoidance of 'contamination' of workers by clients was one reason for the introduction of formalised social work education in the late nineteenth and early twentieth century, so too it is hoped that evidence-based practice, with its claims of ideological neutrality and scientific objectivity, can play a similar role in assisting social workers towards becoming primarily experts in controlling risky individuals and managing behavioural change, less concerned with issues of inequality or oppression.

But the 'What Works' agenda is also political in another sense. There is growing concern within the research community that the evidence on which government seeks to base social policy and legislation may sometimes have less to do with its intrinsic merit than with the extent to which it fits existing or proposed government policies. As an example, in

1999, the British Government committed over £250 million to the Crime Reduction Programme in England and Wales, as an initiative in 'evidence-based policy' aimed at finding out 'What Works'. A major component of this was the Reducing Burglary Initiative. A team led by Tim Hope, Professor of Criminology at Keele University, was successful in gaining a contract to evaluate the cost effectiveness of twenty-one 'Strategic Development Projects' (SDPs) within the Reducing Burglary Initiative (Hope, 2004). At the end of the evaluation, Hope notes that

> Even though our research found much that was interesting and informative about burglary reduction in the community (Hope, et al., 2004), it did not come up with an impressive validation of the SDPs. Although reliably based on our methods, the research estimated that only seven out of the 21 SDPs achieved a significant impact on burglary – including one project that appeared to have produced an increase in burglary in its target area. (2004: 295–6)

However, when two Home Office Research Reports subsequently appeared which made use of the burglary data which Hope and his team had supplied, the analysis of the data presented differed substantially from their own, as did the inferences and interpretations made. The data had, apparently, been passed to other academic researchers for 're-evaluation', and they had been able to reach rather different conclusions from those arrived at by Hope and his colleagues. Some sense of this different emphasis is evident in the Home Office release which accompanied the publication of the Findings. It was headed *Groundbreaking Projects Crack Burglary* and reported the Minister as saying:

> The Home Office has today published an evaluation of its Reducing Burglary Initiative which...has resulted in fewer burglaries...with the help of the Reducing Burglary Initiative, communities across Britain have benefited from a 20 per cent drop in Burglary ... anti-buhrglary strategies have had a tremendous impact on burglary rates. The evaluation published today will help more areas cut burglary by sharing methods. (Quoted in Hope, 2004: 297)

In his review of what was presumably a painful process, Hope shows convincingly that the methods used by him and his team were superior to those used by other researchers. His more general point, however, is to illustrate what can happen when responsibility for validating policy is placed by policy-makers in the hands of social scientists but the evidence produced is not congenial to those same policy-makers. In that situation, he suggests, political pressures may tempt them to 'pretend it works' (in the title of his paper). While it is difficult to assess how common examples like this are (though anecdotal accounts suggest they are not an infrequent occurrence), it does raise questions about the integrity of the 'What Works' project and suggests that, in social work, social policy and elsewhere, what we may be witnessing is not so much 'evidence-based policy' as 'policy-based evidence'.

4

The Market and Social Care

Introduction

In January, 2004, the European Commission adopted a draft Directive on Services in the Internal Market laid before it by former European Commissioner Frits Bolkestein (hence popularly known as the 'Bolkestein Directive'). According to its author, a Dutch liberal politician, the innocuous-sounding aim of the Directive was to establish a legal framework to facilitate the freedom of establishment of service providers in Member States and the free movement of services between Member States. The proposal therefore aimed to remove all barriers to the effective exercise of these two 'fundamental freedoms' of the EC Treaty (European Commission, 2004). In reality, as campaigners against the Directive pointed out, if adopted, it would result in the commercialisation or privatisation of *all* services within the Union, and the opening up to competition of essential sectors such as culture, education, health care and social services. In addition, since the Directive included a 'country of origin' clause which would have allowed companies to use the rules of their home country when setting up shop in another Member State, including paying (often far lower) local wages, it was seen as an attack on workers' rights and conditions (Fritz, 2004).

The resulting opposition to the draft Directive, fuelled by the huge 'Non!' vote in the referendum on the French Constitution in 2005, meant that when the Bill had its first reading in the European Parliament in February 2006, some of its most far-reaching proposals were defeated. To the dismay of business lobbies, and due in part to a massive European trade union campaign against the Bill, cross-border liberalisation will now exclude postal services, temporary employment agencies, health care, legal services and some, though not all, social services such as childcare (*The Guardian*, 17 February 2006). Nevertheless, despite these amendments, it still seems likely that the Bill will become law when it has its final reading in the European parliament in 2010.

In relation to social work and social care, the Bolkestein Directive can be seen as the culmination at a European level of the process that began in the UK with the changes introduced by the 1987–92 Conservative government, particularly through the NHS and Community Care Act of 1990. In that Act, the Thatcher/Major government sought to introduce a business culture and business practices into the realm of health and social care, with the aim of promoting the growth and development of a 'flourishing independent sector'. Here, as in other areas of health and social care in the 1990s, the likelihood of popular opposition to the introduction of the profit motive into health and social care, so contrary to the aims and values of the NHS in particular, meant that the terms used to describe the process – 'the mixed economy of care', the 'empowerment of service users and carers' and so on – were of necessity opaque and misleading. In this connection, as Harris notes, the use of the term 'independent sector' was particularly significant:

> It was a new term that embraced both commercial organisations and voluntary organisations, collapsing some of the previous distinctions between them and cloaking the embrace of the profit motive through use of private sector social services provision. As a result, the composition, management style and ethos of voluntary organisations were constrained to change. (Harris, 2003: 155)

Chapter 3 explored the ways in which these market mechanisms have transformed professional social work. In this chapter, I will explore the impact of these same market forces in the broader sphere of social care services, both for those who use these services and for those who provide them. This will involve looking first at the ways in which the roles of both the private and the voluntary (or Third) sector have changed since the early 1990s, during which time the term 'social care', like the 'independent sector' a term seldom used a decade ago, has come to cover both of these areas of service provision. Has the introduction of competition between providers led to the increased choice, quality, independence and empowerment for service users which the advocates of these changes promised it would? Or has it resulted in a 'race to the bottom', with services and staff conditions being sacrificed to the requirement to secure contracts? Individualised budgets can be seen as representing a further, and more radical, extension of the withdrawal of the State from the provision of services. In the UK, the main form which such individualised budgets have taken over the past decade is direct payments (DPs). In the final section of this chapter, I will continue the discussion of personalisation and personalised services begun in Chapter 3, by considering the extent to which such payments through DP, in part the product of campaigning by disabled service users themselves, should be seen as a 'friend or foe' of people requiring services (Spandler, 2004).

Growing the Private Sector

Prior to the 1980s, the private sector played a small role in the provision of social care in the UK, smaller not only than local authority provision but also voluntary sector provision (Hardy and Wistow, 1999). The main reasons for this were both ideological and financial. On the one hand, until the advent of neo-liberalism, the idea that the profit motive should have a role to play in meeting people's basic health and social care needs was anathema to pretty much everyone, other than a small number of individuals on the outer reaches of the Conservative Party (Timmins, 1996). On the other, the dominance of local authority provision, the fact that most of those who required such provision usually had limited incomes, and the nature of the care involved made the sector relatively unattractive to those seeking opportunities for profitable investment. That situation changed in the 1980s, for two main reasons. First, there was the massive (and unplanned) growth of the private sector as a provider of residential care for older people. This had nothing to do with the merits of the private sector vis-à-vis other forms of provision, nor was it a deliberate consequence of government policy (which was in fact emphasising the merits of older people remaining in their own homes). It resulted, rather, from the exploitation by the residential home care business of a change in social security regulations by the Conservative government in 1980 which meant that the social security system paid the board and lodging costs of older people with assets under £3,000 – in effect, government subsidisation of private residential care. This 'perverse incentive' meant that between 1979 and 1990, the number of places in private residential homes for older people increased from 37,000 to 98,000 while public funding of residential care between 1982 and 1993 rose from £39 million to £2.57 billion (Hardy and Wistow, 1999: 53; Harris, 2003: 41). Meanwhile, domiciliary provision was growing much more slowly.

Government anxiety about growing public expenditure on residential care for older people led them to invite Sir Roy Griffiths to 'review the way in which public funds are being used to support community care policy and to advise the Secretary of State on the options for action which would improve the use of these funds as a contribution to more effective community care' (Griffiths, 1988: 1). Griffiths' recommendations provide the second main reason for the growth of the private sector in social care over the past decade and a half. Under his proposals, the primary role of local authorities would shift from being providers of care to being commissioners and purchasers of care within an expanding social care market. Lest there be any misunderstanding as to what Griffiths had in mind, he was explicit in arguing that 'the onus in all cases should be on social services authorities to show that the private sector is being fully stimulated and encouraged, and that competitive tenders or other means of testing the market are being taken' (Griffiths, 1988: para 24). These proposals were duly incorporated into the 1990 Act, with the government also requiring (in England and Wales) that 85 per cent of the transferred funding be spent on the services of 'independent' service providers.

Not surprisingly, the decade which followed saw a transformation in the provision of social care services. By the end of the 1990s, only 22 per cent of the residential care market remained in the public sector (for the UK as a whole), compared to 63 per cent in 1970 and 39 per cent in 1990. Across the whole range of care accommodation, 81 per cent of residents were in 'independent' facilities compared to 61 per cent in 1990 (Knapp et al., 2001: 289).

At the time of the introduction of the 1990 Act, there was some scepticism amongst social care professionals as to whether the private sector would regard the domiciliary market as sufficiently profitable to merit substantial investment. In fact, the independent sector's share of this market has grown even faster than it has in residential care. In 1992, only 2 per cent of home care hours were purchased from the independent sector. By 1999, that proportion had increased to 51 per cent, almost all of it from the private sector (Knapp et al., 2001: 289–90).

A feature of the residential home care sector in the 1980s was that it was made up mainly of small home proprietors. Two decades later, the changes introduced by the 1990 legislation, and especially the requirement to compete, have resulted in a smaller number of bigger providers, due mainly to the behaviour of local authorities who preferred the economies of scale that only larger providers can offer. Knapp and his colleagues note that while in 1997 organisations operating three or more homes accounted for only 26 per cent of all home care provision, by January 2000

Just 18 large (mainly quoted) companies together operated 1,360 homes, roughly 22 per cent of all private sector UK provision. Interestingly, in view of concerns expressed by some purchasers that larger homes are associated with poorer quality care, mean home size for these corporate bodies was 54 beds, substantially larger than elsewhere. (Knapp et al., 2001: 292)

As an example of the type of provider which is increasingly dominating the social care, consider Four Seasons Health Care, part of the giant Alchemy conglomerate.

According to the company website, founded in the late 1980s Four Seasons now owns and operates approximately 440 nursing and care homes and specialised care centres in England, Scotland, Northern Ireland and Isle of Man (www.fshc.co.uk). The firm cares for over 18,500 people at its care and nursing homes and employs over 21,000 staff. The Care Homes Division comprises approximately 250 homes in England, 50 in Scotland and 60 in Northern Ireland and the Isle of Man. Many types of care are provided in the division's facilities including care for people who are elderly and either frail or mentally infirm. In addition, there are dedicated services for respite care, rehabilitation, intermediate care, terminal and palliative care as well as care for younger persons suffering from chronic conditions. Also, under the Huntercombe Group name, the Specialised Services Division comprises units catering for conditions such as mental health and addictions, physical and neurodisabilities, brain injury rehabilitation and children's services. The company also owns, as a landlord, another ninety care homes. By any criterion, Four Seasons is a major provider but it is not alone. BUPA Care, for example, operate 245 homes and care for over 15,000 residents while a little further down the scale, Care UK provide care and support for over 2,900 people in 90 community-based care homes and independent hospitals and employs over 8,500 staff (www.bupacarehomes.co.uk; www.careuk.com).

Arguably, this rapid growth in the private provision of social care might not be a problem if it could be shown that it had led to significant improvements in the quality of life of those using residential or home care services. In fact, however, the opposite appears to be the case. First, as mentioned above, there is the issue of the size of residential care homes. The critique of 'warehousing' models of institutional care was one of the key arguments in favour of community care in the 1950s and 1960s. Yet the increased involvement of the private sector in social care has led not to smaller-scale provision but the opposite:

> Before corporate for-profit operators entered the industry the average care home in the UK had around nineteen beds. By 2001 the average had risen to thirty. In corporate-owned *nursing* homes – as opposed to residential homes – the average number of beds is now fifty-one, compared to an average of thirty-eight for all nursing homes. The larger the home the more profitable it is, since larger care home operators have access to greater revenues and are able to generate economies of scale. But from the residents' point of view larger homes may tend to detract from the quality of care and contribute to a sense of institutionalisation. (Pollock, 2004: 188–9)

Second, there is the issue of quality of care. In a profit-making industry, where profit margins are tight, there is constant pressure to drive down costs. This has obvious implications for staff wages, workload and training, and consequently for the quality of care provided to residents (UNISON, 2006). Pollock cites one voluntary organisation which has suggested that 'Treating care homes as a financial investment means residents may be seen as a drain on resources' (Pollock, 2004: 190). In the most extreme cases where care homes fail to make a profit, then they are likely to close, with often elderly or vulnerable residents forced to leave what may have been their home for years and seek alternative accommodation. One estimate suggests that by 2003, around 74,000 care home places had been lost across all sectors since 1996, with some 800 homes closing each year from 2000 to 2003 (Pollock, 2004: 190). Given that continuity of care is usually seen as a core element of good practice in the care of older people in particular, this is hardly a recommendation for the sector. In addition to the trauma for elderly residents resulting from closure, a report by the Personal Social Services Research Unit also notes that a

> specifically market induced problem in terms of quality is the time around a 'voluntary' home closure. This is a time when standards can fall dramatically as staff leave and there is evidence of inconsistency and confusion about responsibilities and practice during the process. (Netten et al., 2005: 5)

One factor affecting quality of care which is often cited by care home concerns their relationship with local authorities. In most areas, these are still the biggest commissioners of residential and home care services. However, central government funding to local authorities over the past decade has not kept pace with the rise in demand, with the result that private providers (and, as we shall see below, voluntary sector providers) commissioned to provide services are expected to do more for less, putting further pressure on their profit margins. According to one study, in 1997 a fifth of residential care providers were seriously considering leaving the market, many forced into reducing costs, while overall more than half claimed that prices did not cover costs (Knapp et al., 2001: 293) (though less charitably but plausibly, Pollock has suggested that many of these providers sold their care homes during these years primarily to cash in on the property market boom in these years, especially in the southeast of England – Pollock, 2004: 190).

'Elephants and Mice' – Transforming the Voluntary Sector

If the expansion of the private sector in health and social care has been constrained to some extent by the (still) widely held view that people's basic needs for health, housing and social care should not constitute a source of profit, no such perceptions have held back the growth of the voluntary (or Third) sector. This sector has grown dramatically in recent years in Britain. As Dean (2005) notes:

> In the last decade, the number of charities has risen from 98,000 to 166,000, backed up by a further 200,000 community and neighbourhood groups. The number of professional staff employed has grown to 1.5 million while the number of volunteers is estimated to be 6 million. In a typical year 6,000 new charities are born. Expenditure on services, advocacy and campaigning has almost doubled to £20bn and assets now total £70bn.

The Third Sector already provides over 40 per cent of personal social care and 37 per cent of charities funding comes from the state (via contracts for service delivery) (Dean, 2005; Robb, 2005). As Richard Gutch, CEO of Futurebuilders England (a Home Office backed non-profit organisation) notes, some people continue to perceive the sector

> in terms of volunteers and fundraising. In reality, it involves highly committed staff and trustees negotiating public service delivery contracts with local authorities, primary care trusts and a host of other public agencies. (Gutch, 2005)

However, while the expansion of the voluntary sector into new areas of social care might be seen as less objectionable than the growth of the private sector, in reality the same ideological, legislative and policy drivers are in operation in both spheres. The out-sourcing of local authority services, the introduction of market (or quasi-market) mechanisms, and, above all, the shift from unspecific grant to contract as the basis of funding, were all key elements of the Conservative Government's 1990 NHS and Community Care Act. The result is that Third Sector organisations increasingly act like businesses and compete for contracts with for-profit organisations – they are (often despite their intentions) the 'soft face' of the privatisation of public services and, in particular, the social care sector.

The enhanced role of the Third Sector has both continued and intensified under New Labour. At a Three Sectors Summit in July 2006, for example, attended by (then) Prime Minister Tony Blair and five other Ministers, the Minister for the Third Sector, Ed Miliband, announced that

> The relationship between government and the third sector is evolving as public sector delivery changes to better meet the complex needs and rising expectations of individual users. The third sector is uniquely positioned to make sure that local users experience public services that are specially tailored to meet their needs. The role of the Government will be to enable voluntary organisations to deliver services in partnership with the public and private sectors, bringing with them a more intimate knowledge of user needs, the ability to engage hard–to–reach groups in society, and the capacity to innovate in response to unique local combinations of delivery challenges. (www.theequalitiesreview.org.uk)

Central to this new role is the requirement that voluntary organisations become more 'business orientated'. They are under pressure to operate 'full cost recovery' and to compete against the private sector on a 'level playing field'. According to Helen Tridgell, Director of External Affairs at the Disabilities Trust, for example,

> Businesses and charities are remarkably similar those days. The days of charities being soft and fluffy have long gone. They are just as focused and tough as companies. (Plummer, 2006)

The consequences of this very different role for voluntary organisations have been far-reaching, both for the organisations themselves and for those who use their services. First, the drive to become more like businesses has led to increasing differentiation within the sector, resulting in the development of what one chief executive has called 'the elephants and the mice' (*The Guardian* Special Supplement, 1 November 2006). A tiny 1.6 per cent of voluntary organisations receive 68 per cent of government funding for service delivery, whilst the smallest and most localised, making up 60 per cent of the sector, account for only 1.4 per cent of the funding. The large organisations strive to become more business like, the smallest struggle to pay rent in local authority-provided accommodation (Dean, 2005).

Second, there has been increasing differentiation within the organisations themselves. The Guardian reported that in 2006, the average voluntary sector chief executive had a salary of around £54,000 with some of the larger voluntary organisations paying significantly higher – up to £136,000. But the same cannot be said of the pay and conditions of many of those who work for voluntary organisations. The local government and health trade union Unison launched a blistering attack against conditions in the sector in 2002. Its London organiser claimed,

> I have recently been negotiating on behalf of Unison with a learning difficulties voluntary sector organisation.... [It was] told by its main purchasers, the London Borough's of Wandsworth and Sutton, that under best value scrutiny their unit costs are too high. As a result they propos[ed] their staff take pay cuts of up to £2,000. (Martin, 2002)

Such cuts in wages and conditions are linked directly to the third, and most crucial, change affecting the operation of voluntary organisations over the past decade. This concerns the central mechanism which governments have introduced to ensure that the core neo-liberal concerns of competition and 'value for money' prevail in the Third Sector – namely, the shift from (unspecific) grant to contract. The result has been, as Harris has argued, that

> What were previously understood as relationships of reciprocity between local government Social services Departments and the voluntary sector, were converted into exchange relationships – the voluntary sector was to engage henceforth in direct exchange, for cash, of specified activities or outputs with the social work business. (Harris, 2003: 158)

The way in which the increased reliance on government-funded contracts has impacted on voluntary organisations, particularly smaller ones, was highlighted in a report in 2005 by the British Association of Settlements and Social Action Centres (Bassac, 2006). The report was based on a survey of its members aimed at examining the impact on them of the Treasury's cross-cutting review of 2002. Of 55 members interviewed, 58 per cent said funders had reduced the number of grants used to support community-based activities during this period, replacing them in almost all cases with commissioned contracts and service level agreements. As a result, 73 per cent of respondents said it was now much harder for them to be sustainable and 50 per cent said they felt their independence had been compromised. Rather than devising local solutions to local problems, they were increasingly forced to compete for contracts to deliver centrally devised programmes. Forty-two per cent felt they were becoming less community-based, despite government rhetoric that community-based organisations were central to neighbourhood renewal. Commenting on the Report, Ben Hughes, Chief Executive of Bassac said that

> The move away from grant funding is reducing the type of work that community organisations are able to carry out and instead they are increasingly becoming service delivery agents designed to fulfil the government's target-driven priorities.

Similarly, Julie Corbett, Director of the Blackfriars Settlement noted that

> The contradiction is that the government's own civil renewal agenda promotes neighbourhood hubs and boosting active citizenship. And yet the contract culture lends itself only to larger national voluntary organisations, which mean smaller organisations could find themselves being squeezed out over time. (Bassac, 2006: 4)

Nor is the experience of Bassac an exceptional one. *Stand and Deliver: The Future of Charities Delivering Public Services*, a study of almost 4,000 charities published by the Charity Commission in 2007, provides the most comprehensive study to date of the scale and impact on public service delivery of the charity sector (Charities Commission, 2007). The Report found that health and social care provision topped the table for the most common type of service that charities deliver. It also highlighted the extent to which this 'independent' social care sector relies on State funding for its very survival. Thus, 1 in 3 of these charities received a staggering 80 per cent or more of their income from statutory funders, a figure which rose to 2 in 3 for the largest charities with an income above £10 million. Three particular aspects of that funding, highlighted by the Report's authors, are worthy of comment:

First, there is the dominance of short-term funding. The Report found that two-thirds of all funding agreements for public service delivery were for a period of one year or less. As well as making long-term planning difficult or impossible, this also creates huge instability, as staff are constantly having to worry about their future employment, and threatens continuity of care for service users. As the Report's authors commented:

> Appropriate duration is a key element of sustainable funding, so the short-term nature of the majority of current funding agreements is a potential concern. (Charities Commission, 2007: 20)

Second, there is the adequacy of funding. Forty-three per cent of organisations which participated in the study reported that they do not receive the full costs for any services they deliver. In general, the larger, better-run organisations were more likely to achieve full cost recovery, while smaller organisations had to seek out other sources of funding, including donations from the public. Not surprisingly, then, these smaller organisations are much more vulnerable to cuts in government funding.

Third, there is the way in which dependence on government contracts creates 'mission drift' for many of these organisations. More than a decade ago, Mayo predicted that an increasing service provision role for voluntary organisations would limit or reduce their ability to continue to act as advocates on behalf of their clients (Mayo, 1994). Significantly then, in this study only 26 per cent of the respondents agreed with the statement that charities 'are free to make decisions without pressure to conform to the wishes of funders'. The logic of a contract culture will often be that the funding of organisations whose objectives are seen as politically suspect by government or, at least, are not key priorities, will be squeezed. According to the co-ordinator of a London-based project supporting black women who have experienced domestic violence, for example,

> The government has never adequately invested in the women's sector ... . Now that we're living in an era of commissioning and contracts, specialist groups like women's charities are getting pushed out in favour of generic services that can tick as many boxes as possible. (Kelly, 'Depleted women's groups send SOS', cited in *The Guardian*, 21 February 2007)

The dangers inherent in a government strategy of basing more and more social care provision within the voluntary sector were vividly highlighted in Scotland in early 2007. One Plus was a voluntary organisation set up in the early 1980s to campaign and provide services for lone parents in the West of Scotland. By 2006, it had grown from being a small organisation with a handful of staff to an organisation with an annual income of over £11 million, which employed more than 800 people. It was one of the biggest nursery and out-of-school care providers in Scotland. It had, according to its own publicity, 'over 25 corporate customers, 40 plus streams of funding, 104 individual projects and over 10,000 end-users who are both paying and non-paying'. With justification, it described itself as 'a key participant in Scotland's social economy sector, creating employment, training opportunities and services' (One Plus, 2006).

One Plus went into liquidation on 22 January 2007, following a refusal of continued finding by the Big Lottery and the Scottish Executive (*The Herald*, 8 February 2007). As a result, overnight hundreds of children in the poorest areas of Glasgow lost their childcare places while 600 low-paid, mainly women, workers lost their jobs. Concerns about the financial management of the organisation were cited as the reason for the refusal to provide continued funding, with a Scottish Executive spokesperson stressing that the problems were 'particular' to the organisation and confirming that that the voluntary sector continued to be a 'key delivery agent' in meeting anti-poverty targets in Scotland (*The Big Issue in Scotland*, 1–7 February 2007). Until the Office of the Scottish Charities Regulator has completed its inquiry, the exact reason for the collapse will remain unclear. As one expert, however, who did not wish to be named, noted in an interview with the *Big Issue in Scotland*, the government 'was relying on such organisations to help deliver their promises and that – as the collapse of One Plus had shown – they were not providing enough support to groups that have grown very large, very quickly.' Lack of core funding was also identified in the same article by Hilary Long, Convenor of the One Plus Board (and a senior Scottish social worker), as the real reason the organisation collapsed. For Long

> It was never easy to collect fees from people who often had to choose between paying them or getting new clothes for their kids ... [No core funding from the Executive meant] there were no funds to draw on when we tumbled into crisis.

Individualising Care – Direct Payments and Individual Budgets

So far in this chapter, we have considered the ways in which the development of a market in social care has transformed the roles of both the private sector and of the voluntary, or Third, Sector. In this section, we shall consider an area of care which is experiencing a similar, or even greater, transformation: individualised (or *routed*) care, the main vehicle for which in the UK context is DPs (Ungerson, 2004). An Act introducing DPs schemes for people with disabilities was passed in 1996, with subsequent legislation extending DPs to other service user groups. These schemes involve social service departments in giving money directly to individuals to buy the support they have been assessed as needing, in lieu of the provision of services. They are, therefore, a good example of the personalised services discussed in the Chapter 3. As such, they highlight perfectly the ambiguities and contradictions of current social care policy in terms of their seeming ability to simultaneously promote the empowerment of individuals *and* the withdrawal of State responsibility for the provision of care. Unsurprisingly, therefore, much of the debate around DPs has concerned whether they are best seen as 'friend' or 'foe' of people with disabilities and other eligible service user groups (Spandler, 2004).

The argument that DPs are primarily a source of empowerment comes from two main sources. First, DPs, and individualised budgets more generally, are a central component of New Labour's plans for the future of social care and figure prominently in the 2005 Green Paper for England and Wales *Independence, Well-being and Choice*. According to the (then) Health Secretary John Reid

> Individual budgets will put a stop to the revolving door of care and care assistants because they will allow people to purchase the care they want. They will be able to choose their own carer or instead of receiving institutional care, opt to go for a holiday that will benefit them, and their families in other ways. (Department of Health, 2005)

Such payments, then, sit comfortably with New Labour notions of choice, flexibility and the service user as consumer.

Alongside this governmental support, however, the call for DPs has also been a central campaigning demand of disability activists for more than two decades, as they are seen as a means of gaining greater control over their lives. Indeed, such campaigns were a major reason for the introduction of the 1996 Act (Oliver and Campbell, 1996; Leece, 2004). Given that many such activists would be fiercely hostile to other key aspects of New Labour's welfare reform agenda, including cuts in welfare benefits and the privatisation of services, how compatible are the arguments of these rather strange bedfellows?

In fact, given the history of paternalist, often oppressive and sometimes abusive institutionalised service provision, the attractions of DPs for people with disabilities (and subsequently, elderly care users) are not hard to see. They seem to offer a degree of independence, control, choice and flexibility often lacking from local authority-provided services, as the following example shows:

> I mean, we have to have these carers and it's better than having social services that come in at a certain time and treat you like you're robots – you get up at a certain time, go to bed at a certain time and you function at a certain time. Whereas [with] your own carers, to a certain extent you have got control of what time you want to get up, what time you go to bed, things like that. You say, people say to us, 'Whatever do you want to get up at six o'clock in the morning for?' Well we say when we've been out to bed at half=past ten the night before, we can't move about at all in bed, we can't go to the loo and things like this, so we're ready to get up and move about at that time, you see. (Quoted in Ungerson, 2004: 203)

This focus on choice and control, rather than illness and disability, also means that they can be seen as embodying a social, rather than a medical, model of health and disability. As Beresford and Croft comment:

> Mental health service users, people with learning difficulties and those with physical and sensory impairments, have become able, through direct payments schemes and support from local disabled people's organisations, to recruit their own personal assistants and for these to be solely and directly accountable to them, enabling them to transform their lives by accessing new educational and social opportunities. People who, in the past, would never have conceived of being capable of 'living in the community' are now doing just that in large and increasing numbers. (Beresford and Croft, 2004: 63–4)

Such forms of individualised care appear, therefore, to provide a glimpse of how services could be organised differently, in ways which genuinely reflect the needs and wishes of those who depend on them. At the same time, however, they raise a number of concerns. First, there is the context in which they are being introduced. As we have seen in previous chapters, this is a context of managerialism and marketisation in which the drive to reduce public spending and to extend market forces into all areas of health and social care override all other considerations. That context has far-reaching implications for the way in which such individualised budgets operate in practice. There is, for example, the question of the sums involved. In principle, there is no set financial limit on the size of DPs (Lewis, 2005). In reality, however, such payments will be determined by the state of local authority budgets, with a British study in the late 1990s showing that social service budget constraints had led to the imposition of ceilings on the expenditure on individual community care packages (Kestenbaum, 1999). In its guide to DPs, the Social Care Institute for Excellence accepts that

> It is up to the local authority to decide on the amount of a direct payment, but it must be enough, taking into account any contribution which the individual is

expected to make to the cost of his or her care package, to enable the recipient legally to secure the relevant service to a standard which the local authority considers is acceptable. (Lewis, 2005: 17)

In fact, as Lewis and also Spandler (2004) note, there is evidence that local authorities have seen DP schemes primarily as a means of saving money, to the extent that the lure of cost-cutting has been one of the main attractions of DPs for them.

A second concern is the complexity of managing and administering a payment through the DP scheme. Often, this will involve recipients in opening a dedicated bank account (not a straightforward task for those living in poorer areas, given discriminatory banking policies), submitting monthly statements and returns, and frequently taking on the responsibilities of being an employer. Not surprisingly then, as one study of DP users in Wiltshire showed, even those enthusiastic about some aspects of DPs were clear that there were definite limits to this form of service provision:

> It (DP) is very flexible and meets my respite needs – freedom, but I would not want the responsibility of using a direct payment to meet all my needs as it would be too stressful. (Quoted in Carmichael and Brown, 2002: 802)

For another respondent in the same study:

> There may be a total of five or six personal assistants on my support team, three of whom will be local ... scheduled into the routine are regular house meetings coupled with recruiting new assistants. I figure I spend a good day and a half a week administering the household. (Quoted in Carmichael and Brown, 2002: 803)

The same study also found that users experienced frequent problems with this particular scheme including late payments into bank accounts, forcing users to borrow money from relatives to pay personal assistants (PAs), and conversely, users being penalised for any late submission of returns, which in some cases were due to illness. While the perceived benefits of DP schemes may mean that some users will be willing to accept such drawbacks as the price to be paid for greater independence, such examples also highlight some of the dangers involved in the transfer of risk from the local authority to the individual. The issues of complexity and the stresses involved in administering DPs underpin a third concern over this method of service delivery, namely the extent to which DPs may actually maintain or widen inequalities amongst service users, since clearly those who are more educated, articulate and middle class, may be more able to take advantage of the opportunities offered through DPs. One study found that half of the sample using DPs had previously run their own businesses (Quoted in Leece, 2004: 219), while another found that of forty-one older DP users, many had managerial or supervisor career backgrounds (Clarke et al., 2004).

Fourth, there is concern that the individualisation of service provision which DPs involve can lead to the undermining of collective service provision. According to Spandler, within the critical literature in Canada where such payments have been in operation for much longer than in the UK, they have been perceived as 'a threat to a healthy and vibrant public sector that collectively develops best practices and standards in the provision of support' (2004: 195). Where services are individualised, the opportunities for developing such collective best practice are significantly reduced.

Finally, there are the implications of DP schemes for those who provide the care. To date, most of the literature has focused on the extent to which such schemes, however they are described – independent living, personal budget schemes, DPs – empower service users and increase their independence. Less attention has been paid, however, to their implications for care providers. To address this issue, Ungerson and her colleagues carried out a five-country European study to investigate how far care-workers and care-givers are, or are not, rendered independent or empowered by what she has previously described as the 'commodification of care' (Ungerson, 1997; Ungerson, 2004). Five variants of commodified care were identified: fully commodified 'informal' care (Holland); regulation plus credentialism (France); DPs (UK); additional income into household (Italy and Austria); and undocumented 'grey market' carers (also Italy). Here, the focus will be on the UK findings. According to Ungerson, the general picture is that

> With a direct payments system, care-users and care-workers operate in a labour market characterised by low wages and few skills and qualifications, and in which the organisation of care work (as through agencies) may be rudimentary or non-existent. (Ungerson, 2004: 202)

As one might expect in a system where, consistent with an ethos of consumerism, care-users and care-givers are left almost entirely to their own devices in terms of how they recruit and organise care; the researchers found a very wide variety of 'solutions' and relationships, which might or might not increase independence and empowerment. From the small UK sample, they found some evidence that the scheme gave individual care-users the ability to control both who provided care and the type of care provided. To that extent, they did increase independence and empowerment. The picture from the care-providers, however, was more mixed. Some clearly enjoyed their work and, in particular, the personal relationship they were able to form with the service user. Some talked about becoming 'part of the family'. The downside of that, however, was that some service users felt that they could call on the workers outwith contractual hours, sometimes without payment, with workers feeling that they were at the 'beck and call' of the service user. Ungerson concludes:

> For these workers, it was often a matter of luck whether they had a 'good' employer or not. The fact that they were frequently working alone with no colleagues, and operating in a segment of the labour market which credentialism has hardly touched, meant that they were vulnerable to exploitation based in emotional blackmail. Their independence was hardly enhanced and their power was minimal (as demonstrated by one employer who appeared to sack employees on a whim). (Ungerson, 2004: 204–5)

Concerns about recruitment, employment and training of PAs, as well as the ability of the market to meet the level of demand, have also been raised by Scourfield (2005). In a review of research in this area, he found that finding PAs was a common problem for many service users, mainly due to the low rates of pay that their DPs allowed them to offer. Their biggest problems were unsuitable applicants, competition from other providers and insufficient applicants (Scourfield, 2005: 478). In relation to the first point, Scourfield notes both that PAs are exempt from the scope of the General Social Care Council's register of people working in social care and also that DP users cannot gain access to the Criminal Records Bureau. The increased potential for abuse of the service user within such an unregulated market is obvious. In relation to the third point, he cites an extract from the website of the National Centre for Independent Living:

> Just what type of person would take up working as a PA, given the pay, unsocial hours, lack of training and given the attitude that despite providing a service to the community, to fellow human beings they appear to rank lower than a domestic cleaner, let alone a shelf stacker in the commercial sector? (Scourfield, 2005: 478–9)

The answer would often appear to be those with few other options. Home Office figures collated by the *Daily Mirror* relating to the occupations of East European workers in the UK in 2006, for example, show that 12,610 were working in the category 'care assistants, home carers', the eighth highest out of more than seventy categories (*Daily Mirror*, 23 August 2006), with many of them, presumably, working as PAs. No doubt they will often be caring and committed individuals, providing a much-needed service. It is hard, though, to see how either vulnerable service users or vulnerable workers can be 'empowered' or their independence increased through such a free-for-all market. As Scourfield notes, such arguments are not intended to undermine principles of independent living, nor to cast doubt on the abilities of different groups of service users to manage their own lives. They should at least, however, raise questions about the extent to which government optimism about the 'transformative' power of DPs is fully justified (Scourfield, 2005: 485).

5

Consumerism, Personalisation and Social Welfare Movements

Introduction

In 1966, as the civil rights movement in the USA began to gather momentum, the American socialist theorist and activist Hal Draper wrote a small pamphlet entitled *The Two Souls of Socialism* (Draper, 1966/96). Throughout the struggle against capitalism over the preceding 150 years, Draper argued, one of two strategies had usually predominated. The first, and most common, strategy which he called 'socialism from above' was based on the idea that socialism, or indeed any real social change, must be handed down to the grateful masses in one form or another, by a ruling elite not subject to their control. As examples of this approach, Draper cited the experience both of Labour (or Social Democratic) governments in Britain and Western Europe throughout the twentieth century, and also of 'communist' or Stalinist regimes in Eastern Europe since the 1930s and 1940s. Despite their differences, what these ideologies shared, he argued, was a view of the role of the mass of people as essentially passive, notwithstanding the opportunity for citizens in the West to vote every few years for candidates from parties which often pursued very similar policies. Neither of these ideologies, he argued, nor the political practices which flowed from them, had succeeded in producing societies free from exploitation and oppression.

In contrast, Draper's preferred strategy, 'socialism from below', was based on the belief that real change could only be realised through what he called

> the self-emancipation of activized masses in motion, reaching out for freedom with their own hands, mobilized 'from below' in a struggle to take charge of their own destiny, as actors (not merely subjects) on the stage of history. (1966/1996: 4)

Freedom, in other words, could not be 'given' but had to be fought for and won. As Draper emphasised, the distinction did not only apply to socialist change but rather was to be found in every historical situation where people struggled against injustice and to extend their rights:

> Please note that it is not peculiar to socialism. On the contrary, the yearning for emancipation-from-above is the all-pervading principle through centuries of class society and political oppression. It is the permanent promise held out by every ruling power to keep the people looking upward for protection, instead of to themselves for liberation from the need for protection. (1966/96: 5)

Draper's distinction provides a useful starting point for a discussion of the recent experience of people who use social work and other health welfare services, and in particular of the development of what is usually referred to as 'user involvement' or 'user empowerment'. For it is mirrored in the distinction suggested by Beresford and Croft, Barnes and others (Beresford and Croft, 1993; Barnes, 1997) between two models of user empowerment which, though often conflated in both theory and practice, have competed for dominance within British social work and social care services for more than a decade.

The first of these, corresponding to Draper's 'socialism-from-above', is the *consumerist* model of user involvement, enshrined in Britain in the provisions of the NHS and Community Care Act 1990 and in its subsequent guidance. It is a measure of the ambiguities which surround discussion of user involvement that a piece of legislation, whose stated, seemingly radical, aim was 'the empowerment of users and carers' should also have provided the statutory basis for much greater involvement of the private sector in social care.

The second model, corresponding to Draper's 'socialism-from-below', is not in fact a model of 'user involvement' at all, since it is concerned with people not primarily in terms of their relationship with services but rather as citizens who may also, by reason of physical impairment, mental distress, age or for some other reason require to make use of health and social care services. It is usually referred to as the 'democratic' model of user (or citizen) empowerment (Beresford and Croft, 1995) and differs from consumerist models in four key respects: its origins ('bottom-up', emerging out of collective movements rather than 'top-down'), its aims (social change and social justice, rather than simply involvement in services), ideology (a social, rather than an individual or biomedical, model of health and disability) and its methods (often involving collective action, rather than 'partnership' with service providers).

As Beresford and Croft comment in a discussion of liberatory and regulatory tendencies in social work, the interaction between these two models for more than a decade has led to a situation in which

> The contradictory nature of developments can be shocking. The routine experience of social work and social services for many service users may be the same or even worse than twenty or thirty years ago ... . At the same time, there are examples of change that could not even have been conceived in the recent past. (Beresford and Croft, 2004: 63)

It is these contradictions that this chapter will attempt to unpack. The first section of the chapter will seek to assess the extent to which the top-down consumerism of the past two decades might be seen to have empowered service users and carers. Next, I shall outline and discuss the fashionable concept of *personalisation*, which, according to the Scottish Executive, 'needs increasingly to be the philosophy on which social services are founded' (Scottish Executive, 2006a: 6). How seriously should we treat the claim of advocates of personalised services that these represent an advance on, or alternative to, consumerist models in health and social care? Finally, I shall explore what might be called 'user empowerment from below', the contribution to greater participation and improved services over the past two decades made by the 'new social welfare movements' which have emerged during this period (Williams, 1992), focusing particularly on the experience of the mental health users' movement.

Consumerism: A Basis for Social Development?

To what extent, then, and in what ways have consumerist models of user involvement achieved their stated goal of empowering service users and carers? Critics of these models have often been dismissive of government attempts to reconstruct people who rely on health or social care services as 'customers'. In contrast to the lofty ideals of 'consumer sovereignty', it is argued, most ordinary people lack the basic information on which to base meaningful choices about which services to use (Beresford and Croft, 1993: 67). Even where such information and such choices do exist (which, in many areas of health and social care, they do not), it is far from clear that choice is most people's primary consideration, as opposed to geographical proximity, for example, in relation to schools and hospitals (Means et al., 1994: 23). Further, many groups of service users, particularly mental health users or those involved with statutory social work services, lack the power to make choices, which often continues to remain in the hands of professionals, be they medical personnel or care managers (Walsh, 1995: 196–7). Most importantly, however, in the context of a social care market in which the private sector plays a growing role, most people lack the purchasing power to make real choices about the kind of residential care home or form of psychotherapy they would like. They are, in Bauman's phrase, 'flawed consumers' (Bauman, 1988).

In an unusual paper, however, (given that he is best known as a critic of marketisation) Harris has proposed an analysis which, he suggests, offers 'a different story from the one which is conventionally told about the shift from welfare statism to consumerism' (Harris, 2004: 540). Conventional accounts of the transition from welfarism to consumerism, Harris suggests, typically present it as a move from an era of *social development*, a period when the rights and choices of service users were extended, to an era of *social delimitation*, when inequality increased and these rights were curtailed.

This account, he suggests, is flawed in two respects. On the one hand, welfare statism was often guilty of social delimitation in its construction of the client as a passive recipient without rights, in its reliance on professional knowledge and expertise and in its assessment of general, rather than individual, need. On the other hand, Harris argues, there are at least three ways in which consumerist approaches have shown themselves to be capable of social development, as opposed to simply social delimitation.

The Ambiguity of Consumerism

> At first driven politically by reforming governments, consumerism has, nevertheless, connected with wider movements for change and with a range of concerns, from a variety of perspectives, about the experience of service users. (Harris, 2004: 536)

The ambiguity of the language of consumerism – its stress on empowerment, for example – and its accurate identification of the lack of user involvement in traditional welfare services, Harris argues, have led many service user and carer organisations to take the promises of consumerism at face value. Thus, whatever the motives or intentions of the Conservative politicians who dreamt up the policy in the first place may have been, users and carers have been able to exploit the ambiguities within it to raise the profile of user and carers, improve their position and, in at least some cases, to develop services which are more responsive to their needs. In that sense, one effect of consumerism has been to increase the level of involvement of users and carers.

Procedural Rights

Within both traditional social democratic welfare literature and also within radical and Marxist accounts, Harris suggests, an identity of interest is usually assumed between those who use the services and those who provide them (including, in more radical accounts, the scope for 'class-based alliances'). In practice, he argues, that assumption has often led to a neglect of power differentials between workers and service users, and of the potential for conflicts of interest. In contrast, consumerism's construction of the client as customer has led to an emphasis on procedural rights, such as the right to needs-led assessment and new forms of redress such as complaints procedures. He comments:

> Procedural rights are not a substitute for adequate social policies, but they can address the detail of the individual experience of the user of social services, as well as focus attention on policy success and failure. (Harris, 2004: 538)

Attention to Individual Needs

In contrast to the more generalised, professional-driven approaches to need which have characterised traditional welfare responses ('one size fits all'), consumerism's emphasis on 'tailoring' services to individual needs, based on individualised assessment, have not only made it more likely that service users will receive a more personalised service (and in the case of direct payments [DP] schemes, will construct their own package of care) but has also opened up the discussion of different kinds of need, with greater awareness of the cultural dimension to social rights, including rights to recognition and identity, for example.

In relation to Harris's first point, although difficult to quantify, there is no doubt that many more service users and carers are involved in an active way in different areas of health and social care than was the case twenty years ago. 'Top-down' encouragement has clearly been a factor in this. In a pre-election speech in 2004, for example, then Prime Minister Tony Blair emphasised that such involvement would be the centre-piece of welfare reform in a third-term New Labour government:

> I am not talking about modest further reorganization but something quite different and more fundamental. We are proposing to put an entirely different dynamic in place to drive our public services: one where the service will be driven not by the government or by the managers but by the user – the patient, the parent, the pupil and the law abiding citizen. The service will continue to be free, but it will be a high quality consumer service to fit their needs in the same way as the best services do in other areas of life. (Blair, 2004)

Such official support for user and carer involvement has extended to many areas of health and social care. The impact of that involvement on four of these areas will be briefly considered here: government policy and legislation; service development; health and social care research; and social work education.

Government policy and legislation. In some areas, user and carer involvement appears to have had an impact on policy and legislation. Thus, carers' and service users' organisations were involved in the preparation of the Mental Health (Care and Treatment) (Scotland) Act 2003 which came into force in Scotland in 2005 (Rosengard and Laing, 2001). Arguably, that involvement is reflected both in the principles which underpin the new Act and also in several of its provisions, such as advocacy schemes and advance statements which specify how someone wishes to be treated if they become unwell. These are measures which the mental health users' movement had been demanding for some time. Similarly, the provision of direct payments through the Direct Payments Act 1996, discussed in Chapter 4, might also be seen as an example of the progressive potential of 'top-down' consumerism.

Service development. Service user involvement in the development and management of services is a second area where consumerist approaches appear to have had an impact. Service users play an important role in the running of organisations such as People First in the area of learning disability, for example, or in the Clubhouse model in mental health. Consumerist-driven government policy may be seen to have contributed to such service development both by creating a market in care whereby smaller voluntary organisations (in which there is sometimes a higher level of user involvement) can grow and also by encouraging user involvement through local and national initiatives.

Research. Another aspect of government-driven consumerism has been the emphasis over the past decade on service user involvement in policy research and service evaluation. This led, for example, to the establishment in 1996 of Consumers in NHS Research (now called INVOLVE) to promote the development of service users in NHS Research and Development, the rationale being that such involvement would

> lead to research which is more relevant to the needs of consumers (and therefore to the NHS as a whole), more reliable and more likely to be used. If research reflects the needs and views of consumers, it is likely to produce results that can be implemented. (www.invo.org.uk)

Social work education. A formal requirement for the validation of the new social work qualification, introduced within universities in the UK in 2003/2004, has been that these universities provide evidence of the involvement of service users and carers in all aspects of the new degree, including selection of students, the planning of courses, the delivery of teaching, assessment and review, with routes which failed to provide sufficient evidence being denied validation. In addition, an evaluation of a Scottish-Executive funded project (SIESWE Project 3.3) aimed at increasing user and carer involvement in social work education found that where such involvement was properly funded and supported, then it could have a significant impact on student learning, staff development and user empowerment (www.sieswe.org.uk).

In some areas, then, government-sponsored consumerism appears to have made a difference. It is important, however, to retain a sense of perspective and context.

First of all, the nature and extent of the overall impact of consumerist polices is far from clear. The conclusion of a survey of service users and carer involvement by the Social Care Institute of Excellence, for example, was that

> At the moment there is very little monitoring or evaluation of the difference service user participation is making, although there is quite a lot of information about ways that involve service users. There is less information about the effects of participation, so although much is going on, we do not know whether it is leading to a lot of service change, a little service change or no service change at all. (Carr, 2004: 2)

Others are less hesitant. In a discussion of user-controlled services in mental health, Allott concludes that

> Peer-operated services in the UK are few and far between except for a significant number of poorly-supported and under-funded user groups (Walcraft, Read and Sweeney). (Allott, 2005: 330)

One indicator of the degree of change in the level of involvement by service users in the voluntary sector is provided by the Reports of the Charities Commission. Each year the Charity Commission asks all registered charities to explain how they respond to the need of those who use their services and how these service users influence the charity's development. One recent study of the Commission's reports which looked at the ways in which these charities sought to develop meaningful service user involvement found that 'Few appeared to have made a serious effort to create a mechanism that could engage with users' and concluded that

> Although some exceptions exist, there is not much evidence of real opportunities for 'voice' as opposed to 'choice' for those third sector service users. To date the public sector has also failed in this regard but at least has the possibility of building upon the safeguard of a political structure of democratic accountability behind the direct provision of services. Of course, the private sector makes no pretence at any obligation to involve service users in the design or running of the service. But even among those charities that identify some attempt to create mechanisms to involve service users, it is not clear just exactly an individual service user can become involved. (Davies, 2006)

Of course, service users, workers and local communities have never had as much democratic control over the local and national State as is claimed by supporters of modern Western forms of governance. In that sense, the Welfare State was also guilty of 'social delimitation'. Nevertheless, as I have argued elsewhere, formal accountability represents an important historical victory for citizens within the democratic polity. When money and resources for services are diverted to a range of providers – both the for-profit business and the not-for-profit voluntary organisations – direct accountability is further removed from the democratic process. Accountability becomes reduced to assessment of the extent to which the service provider meets the various targets of service provision; at no point do communities have the right to vote the business or the voluntary organisation out (Lavalette and Ferguson, 2007b).

Harris's second point, concerning the potential for development of procedural rights, is less contentious. At the risk of stating the obvious, since its nineteenth-century beginnings, State welfare under capitalism has never been solely, or even primarily, about meeting human need (Ferguson et al., 2002, chapter two). Historically it has been driven by very different priorities, including the need to control the behaviour of 'risky' individuals or populations (including offenders, or those with mental health problems), the maintenance (usually at subsistence level) of those unable through age, unemployment or disability to sell their labour power, and the need (through family policy) to ensure the reproduction of the future workforce. The recognition that social control continued to be a central feature of the post-war Welfare State, and that the oppression of women, black people and disabled people was built into its very foundations, was the central plank of the radical critique of Fabian paternalism in the 1970s and 1980s (Williams, 1989; Clarke, 1993). These same political and organisational priorities shape and constrain the behaviour of State employees, including social workers, regardless of their individual intentions – both ethical and political – and even allowing for a degree of discretion in the exercise of their professional role. For all these reasons, those who use, or are forced to rely on, State-provided services should as a minimum enjoy basic procedural rights, including access to decision-making forums, complaints procedures and so on.

That said, two factors considerably limit the potential for empowerment contained in such rights. First, the lack of power which most service users enjoy vis-à-vis State employees means that they will often lack the means to enforce these rights effectively. As one study of advocacy schemes within black and ethnic minority populations suggests, while such schemes go some way towards addressing this power imbalance, the evidence for their effectiveness in overcoming the many forms of social exclusion experienced by these service users is at best mixed (Bowes and Sim, 2006). Second, the out-sourcing of local authority services, particularly through the individualised budget schemes discussed in Chapter 4, mean that the scope for even basic redress is likely to become even more limited. The Consultation Document accompanying the Direct Payments Act, for example, was emphatic in insisting that users awarded direct payments would not have access to local authority complaints procedures:

> The recipients will not be able to use this procedure to complain about services purchased as direct payments as these will *not* be the responsibility of the local authority. Nor will personal assistants employed by payments recipients have access to this complaints procedure. *Recipients themselves will need to deal with any disputes arising with the personal assistants they employ or contract with.* (Department of Health, 1995 – my emphasis)

This suggests that the transfer of risk from State to individual which is a central element of consumerism, far from resulting in social development, may curtail even the limited procedural rights which service users currently enjoy.

In principle, the suggestion that consumerist approaches should lead to assessments and services more tailored to individual need, Harris's third point, might seem self-evident, and was in fact one of the main reasons that the 1990 NHS and Community Care Act was welcomed by organisations of service users and carers (as well as by some social policy commentators, for example, Levick, 1992). From the outset, however, whatever empowering potential such assessments might contain has been diluted by the financial context in which they are conducted. As the guidance to local authorities soon after the introduction of the Act made clear (the famous 'Laming letter' – Payne, 1995: 86), local authorities have been permitted to take resource considerations into account when assessing an individual's needs. It was this aspect of the policy which led early critics of the new legislation to suggest that the primary purpose of such individualised assessments had less to do with the assessment of need than with rationing of resources (McLean, 1989; Carpenter, 1994).

If resource constraints impinged on assessments of need in the early 1990s, all the evidence suggest that, more than a decade and a half on, these constraints are felt more, not less, keenly. Thus, a report by the Commission for Social Care Inspection (CSCI) in early 2007 found that individuals and families across England increasingly had to find and pay for their own social care, as two-thirds of councils were now rationing services to people with 'substantial or critical needs' (CSCI, 2007). Commenting on the Report, CSCI chair Dame Denise Platt stated that, faced with increasingly high eligibility criteria set by councils,

> Those who do qualify for care have a high level of need. The options for people who do not meet the criteria set by their local council are limited. In some cases, people rely on friends and family members. In others they pay for their own care. Some people have no option but to do without. (*The Guardian*, 10 January 2007)

Despite these constraints, however, as we saw in the discussion of DPs in Chapter 5, the notion of individualised payments continues to be attractive to many service users, mainly for the reasons that Harris suggests. They are also popular with governments, most recently in the form of 'personalised services'. The next section will consider the potential of this particular variant of consumerism to empower service users and carers.

Personalisation

The most recent development of consumerism within public services is the idea of *personalisation* and *personalised services*. Since 2005, when New Labour began its third term of government, references to 'personalised services' have become commonplace within government publications in the field of adult social care, including the 2005 Green Paper for England and Wales *Independence, Well-being and Choice* and the subsequent White Paper for Community Services in England and Wales *Our Health, Our Care, Our Say*. The latter, for example, promised

> a radical and sustained shift in the way in which services are delivered – ensuring that they are more personalised and fit into people's busy lives. (Department of Health, 2006)

Similarly, for the authors of *Changing Lives*, the result of a two-year long review of social work in Scotland funded by the Scottish Executive:

> Increasing personalisation of services is both an unavoidable and desirable direction of travel for social work services. Unavoidable in the sense that both the population and policy expect it; desirable in the extent to which it builds upon the capacity of individuals to find their own solutions and to self care, rather than creating dependence on services. (Scottish Executive, 2006a: 32)

In its response, the New Labour-dominated Executive went even further in stressing the significance for twenty-first-century social work of this new concept:

> Personalisation of public services, to better match the needs and aspirations of the people who use them, underpins much of current and developing public service policy ... *it is clear that the principle of personalisation needs increasingly to be the philosophy on which social services are founded.* (Scottish Executive, 2006b: 6, my emphasis)

Given that many social workers would be hard-pressed even to define the term, other than the common-sense meaning that services should be more tailored to individual need, this is a fairly astonishing claim. In fact, this lack of familiarity reflects the fact that the term has emerged not from within professional social work or even from service user movements but from a rather more specific source, namely, the influential New Labour think-tank *Demos*. In particular, a ninety-eight-page pamphlet written by former financial journalist and consultant to British Telecom, Charles Leadbetter, entitled *Personalisation through Participation: A New Script for Public Services* (Demos, 2004), has had considerable influence both north and south of the border, to the extent that a paper by Leadbetter and his colleague Hannah Lownsbrough on personalisation and social care in Scotland was subsequently commissioned by the Scottish Executive for the 21st Century Social Work Review (2005).

Since its publication, the original pamphlet has been regularly cited in papers and speeches by government ministers both north and south of the border. An indication of its semi-official status is that it comes with a glowing introduction from Government Minister Ed Miliband, who sees personalisation as a way of overcoming 'the limitations of both paternalism and consumerism' (Miliband quoted in Leadbetter, 2004: 11). So what does this rather innocuous-sounding concept actually mean? Leadbetter introduces his discussion of the concept with a telling comparison:

> Privatisation was a simple idea: putting public assets into private ownership would create more powerful incentives for managers to deliver greater efficiency and innovation. Personalisation is just as simple: by putting users at the heart of services, enabling them to become participants in the design and delivery, services will be more effective by mobilising millions of people as co-producers of the public goods they value. (Leadbetter, 2004: 19)

Leadbetter develops this 'simple idea' by suggesting two accounts of how the public good is produced. In the first account it is produced through the provision of 'top-down', State-provided services. Here, 'the public good goes up the more effective the state becomes in solving society's problems for it'. By contrast, his second – and preferred – account involves a 'bottom-up' approach in which millions of people choose 'to change the way they live, which collectively produces a significant impact in the public good' (2004: 16). To illustrate these two accounts, Leadbetter cites a Department of Health announcement in March 2004, stating that the number of deaths due to heart attacks in England and Wales fell by 23 per cent between 1997 and 2004. Two factors, the announcement suggested, contributed to this fall. First, reforms in National Health cardiac services led to an increase in the number of people taking statins, cholesterol-reducing drugs, reducing the number of premature deaths by 7,000. The second factor, and the one which Leadbetter sees as particularly significant, was lifestyle changes twenty to thirty years earlier when millions of people, encouraged by government, gave up smoking. This, he suggest, points to a model of change in which

[T]he state does not act upon society; it does not provide a service. Instead the state creates a platform or an environment in which people take decisions about their lives in a different way. This is bottom-up, mass social innovation, enabled by the state. (2004:16)

At the same time he suggests that these two accounts need not be contradictory, since the State's capacity to develop better services with limited resources will depend on people becoming more adept at assessing and managing their own health and welfare. To these familiar notions of the 'enabling State' and the 'active citizen', Leadbetter adds a key new concept: the notion of *co-production*. By this he means users behaving as 'active participants in the process – deciding to manage their lives in a different way – rather than dependent users'.

To what extent then does personalisation represent an advance on consumerism in health and social care services? The first point to make is that, though superficially appealing, Leadbetter's 'two accounts' distinction is something of a straw man. Since at least the publication of the Black Report on health inequalities in 1979 (Whitehead et al., 1992), there has been widespread acceptance that health and welfare services play only a relatively small part in the production and maintenance of people's health and well-being. The difference, however, between Leadbetter and earlier researchers such as Black and Peter Townsend is that whereas the latter argued that tackling structural inequalities was key to improving people's health, the central issue for Leadbetter is lifestyle change, with health and economic inequalities barely discussed in either of the two publications, Leadbetter, 1974 and Whitehead et al., 1992, cited above (other than a brief discussion in the penultimate chapter of *Personalisation through Participation* under the heading of 'Obstacles' where he concedes that 'The biggest challenge for the personalised services agenda is what it means for inequality' – 2004: 74).

The implications of that failure to engage with the impact of structural inequalities are clearest in the example which he himself uses. For while levels of smoking have indeed declined significantly over the past three decades, as he acknowledges (2004: 76) this decline is mainly due to the number of middle-class men who stopped smoking two decades ago. The link between smoking and class is, of course, well-established (Blackburn, 1991) and shows little sign of having changed over these decades. A comprehensive study of health and illness in Glasgow and the West of Scotland in 2006, for example, found the lowest smoking prevalence was in the two wealthiest areas of the city (Eastwood and Bearsden) with the estimated prevalence twice this in the four poorest areas of the city (Hanlon et al., 2006). Nor is this an exceptional example. As we saw in Chapter 2, health inequalities in all parts of the UK have continued to grow over the last decade and affect every aspect of people's lives, including their life expectancy (Shaw et al., 2005).

In practice, this means two things. First, the combination of poverty, multiple discrimination, a lack of resources in every sense and (frequently) physical or mental impairment experienced by many users of social work services will significantly reduce their possibilities for making the kind of lifestyle changes recommended by Leadbetter. Through no fault of their own, the average social work client will often not be the 'choosing, deciding, shaping' author of his or her own life whom Ulrich Beck sees as 'the central character of our time' (Quoted in Garrett, 2003: 390). This is not to understate the resilience that many poor people exhibit in the face of oppression and material hardship (Holman, 1998). It does mean, however, that the choices that are available to them will often be very limited, especially for those designated as 'involuntary clients'.

Second, that lack of resources also means that they will often be more dependent on publicly provided services of every type – health, education, social security, social care, transport, housing – than those with private means. In fact most of us, whether through age, illness or unemployment, will be dependent on the State or on other people at some stage of our life, while some of us with chronic conditions are likely to be dependent for a good deal of the time. For that reason, as Stevenson has argued in relation to social work with older people, interdependence is a more useful and less stigmatising concept than dependence (Stevenson, 1989). In contrast, Leadbetter only ever uses the term 'dependent' in a pejorative sense. In a situation where governments across Europe are constantly searching for new ways to force people off benefits and back into work – including in the UK, reducing the number of people claiming disability benefit by one million (Department of Work and Pensions, 2006) – deploring the 'dependence' of service users and emphasising their responsibilities can serve to legitimise policies which users experience not as empowering but as punitive. In practice, such policies will usually involve transferring risk from the State to the individual service user. Despite that danger, in their contribution to the 21st Century Review, Leadbetter and Lownsbrough argue that

> Public policy increasingly needs to shape the choices people make about their lives, to reduce the risk that they will make a costly call on public services by encouraging them to take more responsibility for their actions.... That means people have to shoulder more responsibility for assessing and managing the risks of their own behaviour. (2005: 27)

It is, above all, this view of dependence and independence which makes personalisation theory wholly compatible with the moralism and managerialism which, as we have seen in previous chapters, characterise other aspects of New Labour policy in relation to welfare and social work. At the very least, it should lead us to question that claim that 'the principle of personalisation needs increasingly to be the philosophy on which social services are founded.'

User Involvement from Below: The Experience of Mental Health Service Users

Predating consumerist approaches to user involvement and, as noted above, differing from them in terms of origins, aims, ideology and methods are the collective movements of service users which developed in the 1980s and 1990s. In her study of community care and citizenship, Barnes provides a useful overview of their history and development in respect of people with physical and learning disabilities, mental health service users and older people. As she notes, while these movements have sometimes been dominated by a narrow identity politics (see also Ferguson, 2000), at other times they have shown themselves capable of addressing broader agendas and of developing forms of solidarity with other oppressed groups:

> The significance of user movements thus goes beyond what they are able to achieve to benefit those whose identities and interests are represented directly by such groups, to their potential to act as transformative agents, altering the perspective of dominant groups. (Barnes, 1997: 71)

In particular, the fact that these movements have constructed health and disability as *political* issues, with structural inequality a major determinant of the day-to-day experience of people with physical or mental disabilities, means that they have been able to raise a whole range of issues about power, citizenship and oppression not considered within either biomedical or consumerist paradigms. Here I shall focus on the example of the mental health users' movement (Rogers and Pilgrim, 1991) and assess its impact at three different levels: worker/service user relationships; the content of services; and law, policy and structural oppression. What connects these three levels, I shall suggest, is the analysis of the way in which mental health service users' lives and experiences are shaped by the operation of power, both professional power and State power, and their attempts to regain some control and make their voices heard.

Worker/Service User Relationships

The operation of power within psychiatric relationships is an issue which has often been ignored or denied within medical discourses (Tew, 2006). Yet historically, relationships between people with mental distress and their professional helpers have been characterised by extreme power imbalances. At one end of the spectrum, these have been reflected in an ideological reluctance on the part of these helpers to give credence to their clients/patients' accounts of what they are feeling or what they find helpful. As Lindow notes:

> The most frequent complaint among people who have received mental health services is that nobody listens. Traditional stereotypes combine with current ideas about mental distress, causing a situation in which mental health professionals are trained to ignore the content of what service users say. (Lindow, 1995: 206)

In addition, the fact that, unlike other users of health and social care services, people with mental distress can be compulsorily detained and treated makes these relationships qualitatively different from other forms of helping relationship. As Campbell has argued:

> The psychiatric system is founded on inequality. By and large, the user is at the bottom of the pile. Our unequal position is symbolised by the compulsory element in psychiatric care. I do not intend to argue either for or against the use of legal compulsion in treatment. But the fact of its existence has repercussions for all service users and must be recognised. That an individual can be compelled to receive psychiatric treatment affects each in-patient regardless of whether his stay is formal or informal. (Campbell, 1996: 59)

The growth of the mental health users' movement, as well as the findings of user views' research, has begun to pose new questions about the nature of these 'therapeutic' relationships by exposing the link between power, powerlessness and mental well-being and specifically, the ways in which a lack or loss of power can negatively impact on mental health. Discussing the place of the biomedical model in the development of mental health services, for example, one leading Scottish activist commented:

> That's the model that the users movement was formed to oppose. That's what creates mental illness. Losing sight of personal worth, taking away personal autonomy – that makes mental health problems worse. That model belittles and infantilises. (Quoted in Ferguson, 1999: 173)

The link between power and mental well-being on the one hand, and loss of power and increased mental distress on the other, were recurrent themes in this particular study which was based on interviews and focus groups involving eighty service users. By contrast, a model of service about which many respondents were enthusiastic was the International Clubhouse model which stresses democratic participation and the reduction of power inequalities between workers and users (as well as the role of work in enhancing mental health). Respondents involved in the Clubhouse which participated in the study highlighted the way in which their lack of confidence had been challenged, and their mental health improved, through involvement in Clubhouse roles and activities. Other than the rather evangelical tone (which is sometimes a feature of this organisation), the following comments by one Clubhouse director in England accurately reflect the views of service users and workers in the Scottish study:

> It never ceases to amaze me as I witness the literal transformation that takes place as members discover their roles in the Clubhouse and begin to use their own ideas, talents and abilities to enhance part of the Clubhouse for the benefit of its members. It is as if you can watch the layers of armour shielding them from ignorance, contempt and indifference gradually drop off to expose feelings of power, mastery, confidence and self-esteem. (Quoted in Oliver, Huxley, Bridges and Mohamad, 1996: 210–11)

To date, limited research has been undertaken into the relationship between power (both individual and collective), powerlessness and mental well-being. One suggestive example of the potential for collective action to improve mental health comes from Barker's study of the dramatic rise of the trade union movement Solidarity in Poland in the early 1980s (Barker, 1986). He cites a newspaper report where a doctor describes how in her hospital, following some major victories over the regime by the new union, not only did the working-class patients in her hospital begin to recover more quickly but also the beds they vacated began to fill up with sick *apparatchiks*! (Barker, 1986: 39). As I have suggested elsewhere in a discussion of Marx's theory of alienation, there is considerable scope for researching both the impact of powerlessness on a number of areas, including mental health and also the formation of racist attitudes, as well as the potential of collective approaches for redressing power imbalances and improving the mental health of those involved (Ferguson and Lavalette, 2004).

Services

As Rogers and Pilgrim noted in their early study of the mental health users' movement in Britain (1990), the most common basis for people involving themselves in movement activities was their personal experience both of mental distress and of the psychiatric system. The collective articulation of that experience over the past two decades has given rise to social models of mental health and distress (Tew, 2005), which have in turn underpinned the development of new types of services. These new models and services tend to share three common features. First, there is a recognition of the importance for mental health of power, loss of power and the implications of this for worker/service user relationships. Second, there is an emphasis on the *social* nature of mental distress, from the long-term impact of early trauma to the ongoing impact of structural inequality (Pilgrim and Rogers, 2002; Plumb, 2005). Third, there is a view of mental health and mental distress as a continuum, rather than a 'them' and 'us' separation between the mentally well and the mentally ill. Not only does the latter view misrepresent the nature of mental ill-health but also the social isolation and sense of alienation to which it gives rise is seen as a factor contributing to mental distress.

A range of user-led services and responses to mental distress has developed in the UK over this period, based to a greater or lesser extent on the three features noted above. Three examples will be briefly described here.

Hearing voices. The Hearing Voices Network is based on the work of Dutch psychiatrist Marius Romme (Romme and Escher, 1998). Following involvement in the late 1980s with a patient who stated that she heard voices but did not feel this was a problem, Romme and his patient appeared on a popular Dutch television programme and invited viewers who heard voices to write to them. Of the 450 people who wrote to Romme after the programme stating that they too heard voices, a third stated that they had no difficulty in coping with their voices and of this group, many did not use medication nor had they ever had a diagnosis of schizophrenia. The main difference between those who had received a diagnosis of schizophrenia and those who had not appeared to be that the non-patients saw themselves as stronger than their voices, while the patients did not. According to Richard Bentall, a clinical psychologist who has played a leading role in developing Hearing Voices networks in Britain, aimed at helping voice hearers develop non-medical ways of managing their voices:

> This startling and quite deliberate attempt to move the boundaries of madness demonstrates that even the experiences normally attributed to schizophrenia *do not have to be considered* pathological. It may be true that hallucinations and delusions are found throughout the world, but whether or not these experiences are seen as evidence of illness appears to vary according to local customs and beliefs. (Bentall, 2003: 138)

Two of the three features referred to above are particularly evident in this model. On the one hand, managing the voices increases a hearer's sense of personal agency and power; on the other, the recognition of the widespread nature of voice-hearing (including the discussion of voices in a group setting) reduces the hearer's sense of isolation and difference.

Recovery. The second example, which might be seen as a more general application of the Hearing Voices approach, is the concept of recovery (Allott, 2005). Traditional psychiatry has tended to be fairly pessimistic about the prospects of recovery from serious mental illnesses, despite the substantial empirical evidence of widespread cultural and geographical variations in recovery from conditions such as schizophrenia (Warner, 1994). A growing user literature over the past two decades, however, (with a seminal early text being Chamberlin, 1988) has highlighted not only the limitations of such traditional psychiatric responses to serious mental ill-health (with research in 2006, for example, showing that the new range of drugs for schizophrenia are no more effective than their much older predecessors – Curtis, 2006) but also, and more positively, the many ways in which people actively manage their own mental health problems to the extent that they are often able to lead more or less normal lives. In New Zealand, where the concept of recovery was central to the Blueprint for mental health services introduced in 1998, recovery is defined as:

the ability to live well in the presence or absence of one's mental illness (or whatever people choose to name their experience). Each person with mental illness needs to define what 'living well' means to them.

The Blueprint continues:

most will do much better if services are designed and delivered to facilitate recovery. Virtually everything the mental health sector does can either assist or impede recovery. (Quoted in Allott, 2005: 324)

Such an approach is clearly not without its dangers, since it can lead to mental health being seen primarily as a matter of individual responsibility. On the other hand, the attractions to many service users of an approach which values the coping strategies which they have developed, reinforces their own sense of agency and suggests that mental ill-health need not be the end of the world are obvious.

Crisis services. The third example of new types of service arising out of the experience of mental health service users is crisis services. Dissatisfaction with traditional psychiatric responses to mental health crisis has been a persistent theme in mental health service user literature and discussion since at least the mid-1980s. It is only in recent years, however, that crisis services based on a social model of mental health have begun to develop more widely (Faulkner, 2002; Stalker et al., 2005). Research into crisis services in Scotland found that community-based crisis services, based on a person-centred approach, could play an important preventative role by preventing a 'social crisis', be it financial concerns, family problems or loneliness, escalating into a full-blown psychiatric crisis. While none of the respondents in the study argued for the closure of hospital-based psychiatric emergency services as part of a spectrum of services, all saw having 'someone to talk to', rather than any more medicalised response, as the most important constituent of crisis services. Also important for these service users was the need to remain in control and to experience a sense of agency, something that was often lost following admission to hospital:

> Social crisis [is] very much about the person knowing that they need some support and if they have that support, they could deal with whatever's going on for them.... When people talk about social crisis, to me that implies that the person still retains an ability to be able to influence what's going on. (Stalker, 2005: 23)

The Mental Health Users' Movement

The collective organisation of people who use mental health services is a relatively new phenomenon in Britain. While the politics of mental health, in the form of anti-psychiatry, was one significant element of the 'counter-culture' which emerged in the late 1960s (Roszak, 1969), this was essentially a professional-led movement, albeit one which sought to validate the experience of people with mental health problems (Kotowicz, 1997). In contrast, while the support and involvement of professional allies has been important, the mental health users' movement which has developed in Britain since the mid-1980s has been mainly composed of, and led by, people with experience both of mental ill-health and of the psychiatric system (Pilgrim and Rogers, 1991). Thus, while the basis of the earlier anti-psychiatry movement was an ideological critique of bio-medical understandings and responses to mental distress, in contrast, as Barnes and Shardlow found in their research into the current movement:

> The factors which provide the strongest motivation to participate in mental health user groups are the shared experiences of distress and of being a recipient of mental health services – of 'being a patient'. (Barnes and Shardlow, 1996: 130)

Barnes suggests that the key objectives of these groups are advocacy (both self-advocacy and citizen advocacy); influencing the nature and pattern of mental health services; and the provision of support to their members (Barnes, 1997: 51). Research into mental health users' group in Scotland also found that they involved themselves in a range of material issues, including campaigns against proposed cuts in benefits and in services (Ferguson, 2000).

The obstacles facing the development and maintenance of mental health users' collective organisation are considerable. The still-powerful stigma against mental ill-health makes it much harder, for example, for people to 'come out' than is the case in other social movements. In addition, the realities of professional power and the fear of loss of liberty, plus the loss of confidence arising both from involvement in the psychiatric system and from the experience of mental ill-health do not tend to encourage assertiveness. As a member of one mental health project in Scotland observed:

> I'm here because I've no confidence. You see other people, they say 'G was a union man.' But when you're in the hospital, you depend on the staff to help you, you look up to them. So when it comes to shouting the odds, you've no self-confidence. You can't go out into the street and shout 'I'm daft – what are you going to do about it?' You've had no self-confidence in the first place – you hide away. (Quoted in Ferguson, 2000: 243)

Such challenges to the collective self-organisation of mental health service users and, to varying degrees, other groups of disabled people make it harder for these movements to make the same kind of impact that earlier social movements were sometimes able to. That said, the fact that the collective organisation of mental health service users has survived at both local and national level in the face of such difficulties is a tribute to the courage and determination of all those involved. Not only has it survived, but it also clearly has had some impact. The promotion of anti-stigma campaigns by the Scottish Executive, for example, or the involvement referred to above of service users in the development of new legislation in Scotland, or the growing recognition of the need for a different kind of service response to mental health crises (Stalker et al., 2005) owe at least as much to the campaigning activities of service users as to the operation of a top-down consumerism.

Conclusion

In this chapter, I have suggested that a distinction between *change from above* and *change from below* is a useful way of making sense of service user involvement and also of exploring its relationship to what Harris calls 'social development' – its potential, in other words, for extending rights and powers. Perhaps the main conclusion emerging from the above discussion on consumerism is the importance of locating such forms of involvement in the broader context in which they are being introduced, a context, as we saw in previous chapters, of 'responsibilisation' which makes 'customers' of health and social care services increasingly responsible for the choices that they make. It may be that in pointing to consumerism's scope for social development, Harris is trying to generate some hope in what might otherwise be seen as a fairly pessimistic analysis. What this chapter suggests is that such hope *does* exist, but it is to be found primarily in the gatherings, discussions and campaigns of service users and their allies. It is in the plans and dreams of these fragile but visionary movements that we get a glimpse of just how different relationships between professional social workers and people who use services could be.

6

The Radical Tradition

Introduction: 'The Road Not Taken?'

In a discussion of issues in international social work, Midgley has suggested that three distinct, if sometimes overlapping approaches, have, to a greater or lesser extent, shaped social work practice since its inception (Midgley, 2001). The first of these, *remedial* social work, has historically been the most widely adopted approach to practice. Remedial social work has usually involved direct work with adults, children and families, in fieldwork or residential settings, aimed at addressing the problems they are experiencing, or are seen by others to be experiencing. The remedial, individual focus of this approach has led it to draw primarily on a psychotherapeutic knowledge base, whether psychoanalytic, person-centred or cognitive-behavioural. As Midgley notes, however, this individualism, coupled with a neglect of material issues, has made it the butt of much criticism in recent decades.

The second approach outlined by Midgley is *developmental* social work. In part, this approach arises out of the critique of remedial social work and stresses the need for social workers to engage with processes of economic and social development. Developmental approaches have been important within British and American social work at particular points in history, notably in the Settlement movement in the late nineteenth and early twentieth centuries and again in the late 1960s and early 1970s. However, the shift to the Right in both British and American politics during the 1980s contributed to the marginalisation of community development approaches within social work, while the development of neo-liberal approaches to social work in the early 1990s, leading to the domination of care management approaches, have meant a return to individualistic approaches. In practice this has meant that development, or social development, approaches to social work have been most influential in countries of the Global South, or in countries, such as Canada or Australia, where a more critical tradition has survived (see, for example, Whitmore and Wilson, 2000; Burkett and McDonald, 2004; Kuruvilla, 2004).

The third approach identified by Midgley is the *activist* approach, more commonly known as radical, or structural, social work. As he notes, activist social work has never been a dominant current in social work. More frequently, it has been, in the title of Reisch and Andrews' history of radical social work in the USA, 'the road not taken' (Reisch and Andrews, 2002; Reisch, 2004). But as Midgley notes, 'the profession has since its early days advocated social reform and engaged in activist form of practice' (Midgley, 2001: 29). What we have called the radical kernel of social work has been more evident at particular times and in particular places than at others. In the British context, it can be seen in some of the debates between the leaders of the Charity Organisation Society (COS) and those involved in the Settlements in the late nineteenth century (Mullaly, 1997); in Clement Attlee's 1920 discussion of 'the social worker as agitator' (Attlee, 1920); in the radical social work movement of the 1970s; and in the growth of militant user movements, such as the disability movement and the mental health users' movement, in the 1990s (Thompson, 2002). In the USA in particular, there is a rich and fascinating, if hitherto hidden, history of social work radicalism, best personified in the life and work of the social work educator and political activist Bertha Capen Reynolds, a tradition to which Reisch and Andrews have performed an invaluable service by recovering. Finally, with some exceptions (McLaren and Leonard, 1993; Whitmore and Wilson, 2004), there has been an almost-total neglect within mainstream Western social work of the role played by social work in the struggle for social justice in many Latin American countries, influenced by the ideas of Paulo Freire and by liberation theology.

In presenting this typology, Midgley expresses the hope that the development of an international social work theory and practice which can respond to the issues and challenges thrown up by globalisation may allow for the overcoming of what he calls 'the internecine disagreements which have plagued social work since its formative years' (2001: 30). Given that these approaches are based at least in part on sharply opposing understandings about the nature of the society we live in and the role of social work within it, this is perhaps an over-optimistic aspiration. That said, what is certainly true is that the impact of neo-liberal policies on the lives of service users on the one hand, and on traditional social work practice on the other, is forcing a rethink of the strengths and weaknesses of each of these traditions and is creating a space for the development of new alliances and new forms of practice, based on shared values and a shared notion of what the role of social work could be. Some of these possibilities will be explored in Chapter 8, the final chapter. Before then, however, it is necessary to review the tradition which has been most explicit about the need for social workers to be partisan and to demonstrate their commitment to social change and social justice: radical social work.

Radicalism in Social Work: Some Origins

Within the UK, the emergence of radical social work is usually associated with the ideas and strategies of the movement that developed in the 1970s, whose founding text is the eponymous collection by Bailey and Brake (1975). Certainly the experience of radical social work in Britain during this period was an important one, as reflected not least in the huge amount of analysis which has since been devoted to it (Powell, 2001). There are dangers, however, in associating radical social work too closely with the movement which emerged in Britain in the 1970s. For one thing, an important radical social work literature and practice also emerged during this period in several other English-speaking countries including Canada and Australia, as well as in Latin America, which has been largely ignored within British social work education (Lavalette and Ferguson, 2007a). For another, focusing too narrowly on the 1970s has sometimes led to a neglect of earlier examples of radicalism in Britain and elsewhere, as well as broader social reform currents within social work. One of the main (and erroneous) arguments of conservative critics of radical social work in the 1970s, for example, was that this approach was an alien intrusion into a hitherto politically neutral profession. In fact, social work has seldom been politically neutral. As Powell notes 'Politics was ... in evidence in social work from its infancy and shaped its historic mission into a concern for the poor and the oppressed' (Powell, 2001: 27). For some periods of its history, the dominant politics of social work have been conservative, at other times social democratic, while less frequently, its radical kernel has come to the fore, often in response to radical social movements *outside* social work. To illustrate the point, before discussing radical social work in the 1970s, we shall consider two examples of such earlier radicalism.

Britain 1870 –1920. From its inception in the late 1860s until the First World War, British social work was dominated by an ideology of individualism, which sought explanations of poverty in the character of the individual client, rather than in social or economic structures. As Stedman Jones has argued, the method of casework employed by the COS flowed logically from this ideology, as the primary aim of the 'friendly visiting' carried out by COS volunteers was to ascertain the extent to which individuals were capable of making use of the help which the COS offered (Stedman Jones, 1984: 256–7). Most, apparently, were not: COS returns for 1913–14, for example, show that in that year, less than half of those who sought assistance were helped (Whelan, 2002: 22). Some flavour of the ethos of the organisation can be gathered from a minute of the London Council of the Society which solemnly opined that 'When an applicant is truly starving he may be given a piece of bread if he eats it in the presence of the giver' (Cited in Lewis, 1995: 47). By any criterion, the COS was a highly political organisation. Its leaders consciously saw it as a bulwark against the spread of socialist ideas. Its opposition to almost every progressive measure of the day was no accident but flowed from an ideology which saw casework as

the antithesis of mass or socialistic measures, and the defender of casework finds that his plans will not rest merely on negating socialism but in proving

that there is still much to be said for what can be described as individualism.
(Milnes, quoted in Walton, 1975: 150)

In its fierce opposition to free school meals for children, old age pensions
and national insurance (on the grounds that all of these measures would
undermine 'family responsibility'), the COS richly merited Clement Atlee's
description of it as an organisation 'essentially designed for the defence of
the propertied classes' (Cited in Lewis, 1995: 86).

Such a harsh ideology and practice soon gave rise, however, to a range
of opposing ideas from both inside and outside the nascent profession.
For the most part, that opposition came from Fabians such as Sydney and
Beatrice Webb (Beatrice had herself been a COS visitor), who argued the
need for social reform, as well as from some sections of the volunteer
movements, particularly the Settlement movement, which espoused a more
humanistic worldview than the COS (Harrison, 2004). Such reformist
ideologies brought both the Fabians and the critics of the COS into conflict
with the dominant laissez-faire ideas of the late nineteenth century. Writing
of this period, Powell notes that

> There was a growing sense amongst social workers that there needed to be
> a fundamental reform of the existing political order, and this posed a major
> challenge to the Social Darwinism advocated by the leadership of emerging
> Victorian civil society. (Powell, 2001: 27)

Historians have usually attributed the decline of the COS to a number
of factors including an increased awareness of the real extent of poverty
in Britain following the surveys of Booth and Rowntree, concern
regarding the poor state of the nation's health uncovered through recruitment
attempts during the Boer War and a growing conviction that only social
reform, as opposed to individual voluntary action, could begin to address
social problems. All of these factors were undoubtedly important and
contributed to the landslide victory of the Liberals on a social reform
programme in the 1906 election. Two other, less well-documented sources
of change, however, were also significant in the organisation's decline.

First, there was opposition to laissez-faire ideas from within the COS
and Settlement Movement. While little research has been conducted into
the views and experiences of the 'friendly visitors' who carried out the
casework, there is some evidence to suggest that, despite their middle-class
backgrounds, their direct contact with poor people sometimes led them to
question, and in at least some cases, to reject the official COS ideology. In her
biography of the Member of Parliament Eleanor Rathbone, for example,
Pedersen cites the example of Maude Royden, like many volunteers a
young woman from a wealthy family, who spent eighteen months working
in the Liverpool Settlement:

> She was not judgemental, and some of her encounters would have made the
> theorists of the Charity Organisation Society turn pale. When one docker's wife

confessed that she had squandered every penny of the £300 she had received for her husband's death, Royden thought it was 'grand, that, just for once, she had the chance to do so!' The woman recounted some of the things that she had bought, and she and Maude 'laughed like hyenas'.

Royden was clearly frustrated by the inadequacy of the Settlement's theories and programmes as a means of addressing poverty. She was, she admitted:

'an idiot at grasping the difference between the deserving and the un-!' ... . All of the women looked 'unspeakably poor' to her, and she could understand why they would drink like fiends: 'Poor, poor dears. I should drink if I lived in Lancaster Street'. (Pedersen, 2004: 86)

The introduction of formalised social work education in the early 1900s as a means of combating such 'contamination' of friendly visitors by their clients suggests that such views were not confined to a few individuals (Jones, 1983; see also Harrison, 2000, for Beatrice Webb's experiences of the COS).

A second neglected factor in the demise of the COS – and an important early example of how social work can be shaped by social movements outside its ranks – was the collective action of the poor themselves, and in particular, the London unemployed riots of 1886 and 1887. How to deal with the 'social residuum', the growing ranks of the casual poor, had been a major concern of the London middle classes for some time and an important reason for the establishment of the COS in 1869. That concern came to a head, however, in the mid-1880s when following a trade downturn and two severe winters, London was shaken by mass riots of the unemployed which culminated in 'the battle of Bloody Sunday' on 13 November 1887. As contemporary accounts suggest, this was a police riot, rather than a riot of the poor:

No-one who saw it will ever forget the strange and indeed terrible sight of that grey winter day, the vast sombre coloured crowd, the brief but fierce struggle at the corner of the Strand and the river of steel and scarlet that moved slowly through the dusky, swaying masses, when two squadrons of the lifeguards were summoned up from Whitehall. (Cited in Stedman Jones, 1884: 296)

The response of the local ruling class to such events was twofold: on the one hand brutal repression, on the other, the setting up of the Lord Mayor's Mansion House Fund, which to the horror of the COS, threw all principles of 'scientific alms-giving' to the wind and distributed largesse indiscriminately and on a massive scale to the London poor. One recent attempt to demonstrate the relevance of the philosophy and methods of the COS to dealing with 'the underclass' today, has argued that the negative experience of the Mansion House Fund demonstrates the superiority of COS methods (Whelan, 2002). In fact, as Stedman Jones has argued, it was the riots of the mid-1880s, rather than the excessive generosity of the Mansion House Fund, that sounded the death knell for the COS. For what they demonstrated was the inability of laissez-faire approaches not only to address the problem of poverty (as the experience of the Boer War would soon demonstrate) but also to manage the political 'problem' of the poor:

> While the Society remained obsessed by the demoralizing effects of indiscriminate charity ... the middle-class public was primarily concerned to avert what they conceived to be the imminent threat of an insurrection of the poor. (Stedman Jones, 1984: 300)

That fear was increased by the growth of New Unionism at the end of the decade, which helped to overcome the division between organised skilled workers and previously unorganised casual workers on the other (Charlton, 1999). The overall effect of this movement of the very poorest in society was to hugely strengthen the arguments both of the Fabians and of the COS's critics within the Settlement movement, so that by the end of the decade, the COS 'found itself a defender of what was increasingly coming to be regarded as an esoteric, sectarian and anachronistic social philosophy' (Stedman Jones, 1884: 313). As so often in the history of social work, social movements outside the profession fuelled the developments of more critical currents within.

Radical Social Work in the USA

The experience of early British social work shows both that oppositional currents and ideas were present within social work from its inception, and also the role that movements from below can play in shaping social welfare practices and ideologies (Lavalette and Mooney, 2000). It would be wrong, however, to exaggerate the extent of radicalism in Britain in this period. In contrast to its European counterparts, Fabianism was a peculiarly timid species of socialism, driven at least as much by notions of social imperialism ('improving the British stock') as by a desire to emancipate the working-class (Harrison, 2004). For example, Canon Barnett, the leading figure in the Settlement movement, while critical of the leaders of the COS, was nevertheless prepared to support colonies for the casual poor, arguing that 'it is a shocking thing to say of men created in God's image but it is true that the extinction of the unemployed would add to the wealth of the country' (Stedman Jones, 1884: 304).

In contrast, social work radicalism in the USA in the first half of the twentieth century was a more serious affair. While it did not emerge as an organised current until the 1930s, from the first decade of the twentieth century, social workers appear to have been involved in the social movements of the period, including radical trade unionism, feminism and pacifist movements, in a way which few early British social workers were (Reisch, 2004). For example, while the most famous Settlement

House, Hull House in Chicago founded by Jane Addams, was based on her experiences of living and working at Toynbee Hall in Britain, the atmosphere in Hull House seems to have been decidedly more radical than that of its British counterpart (Powell, 2001). According to Reisch and Andrews:

> The intellectual climate at places like Hull House in Chicago and the Henry Street Settlement in New York, in which radical intellectuals and activists mingled, nurtured the development of radical ideas, including feminism, and created an opportunity for women to expand their intellectual and political horizons. (2002: 25)

While, like many of these early radicals, Addams was influenced by Christian, rather than Marxist or socialist ideas, some sense of the distance between her ideas and those of her British COS counterparts in relation to issues of poverty and 'dependency' is evident in her statement at the 1897 Conference on Charities and Corrections:

> I have not the great fear of pauperizing people which many of you seem to have. We have all accepted bread from someone, at least until we were fourteen. (Cited in Reisch and Andrews, 2002: 26)

The Settlement movement in the USA is one of the best examples of social work as a social movement. By 1910, there were more than 400 settlements in the USA, which were active not only in providing direct help but also in campaigning around issues such as child labour and shorter working hours for women. 'Social workers, regarded by politicians and businessmen as misguided zealots, came to be recognised as the most effective reformers of their generation' (Morrison et al., 1969, cited in Powell, 2001: 39). Moreover, they were actively involved in organising trade unions, enthusiastically supporting strikes and frequently experiencing arrest on the picket line (Powell, 2001: 39).

This radicalism was not without its limitations. There is little evidence, for example, of social work opposition to the racism which, then as now, dominated American society. The doors of Hull House were not open to African Americans, Latinos, American Indians or immigrants from Asia and the Pacific Islands; as Reisch and Andrews note 'The concept of the melting pot was never intended to refer to any groups other than the White ethnics from Europe' (Reisch and Andrews, 2002: 26). Moreover, building links across classes – 'class harmony' – rather than eradicating class society seems to have been Addam's main goal. Even with these limitations, however, the American movement of the first decade of the twentieth century continues to provide an important example of early social work radicalism.

More important, however, in terms of the challenge it posed to dominant notions of social work was the Rank and File Movement which emerged in the 1930s. Drawing consciously on socialist and Marxist ideas, the movement

> challenged the concept of social work as a profession and undermined prevailing notions of social work practice. Unlike their mainstream colleagues, the Rank and File Movement identified with clients, used tactics such as strikes and boycotts, and displayed open sympathy for allied left-wing causes ... . Its leaders played key roles in organised labour and in Popular Front organisations that were affiliated with the Communist Party. (Reisch and Andrews, 2002: 160–1)

The central figure of radical social work and within the Rank and File Movement during this period was Bertha Capen Reynolds. It is significant that while British social workers in the past have been happy to draw on the ideas of other American social work educators such as Florence Hollis or Helen Perlman, Reynolds' work is almost unknown in the UK. Yet during the 1930s, she was the most published social work writer in the USA and for two decades was on the Faculty at Smith College of Social Work, until her blacklisting in 1938. Like radical social workers almost fifty years later (Leonard, 1984), Reynolds was concerned with developing a social work theory and practice that could adequately theorise the interrelationship between exploitative social structures and personal experience. Reisch and Andrews summarise her achievements as follows:

> For the most part, her greatest influence was through her publications and presentations, in which she attempted to integrate Freud, Marx and Rank into a coherent practice framework. Yet, in her professional activities, she also sought to reconcile the Rank and File Movement's desire for structural change in the economy with the potentially ameliorative role of social casework. Reynolds linked the future of casework to recognition of the roots of the Depression in the increased concentration of wealth and the need to create countermovements for democracy, including the decentralisation of social services. (Reisch and Andrews, 2002: 79)

Some of Reynolds's key ideas, such as the notion of mutuality, involving a more equal relationship between workers and clients, as well as her emphasis on prevention, have become part of the vocabulary of mainstream asocial work, albeit stripped of their radical content. The wider movement which she helped to found, however, was crushed, like so many other radical movements of her day, by the onset of the Cold War in the 1940s and the vicious witch-hunt against radicals and radical ideas led by Senator Joseph McCarthy (Reynolds, 1963/1991; Reisch and Andrews, 2002).

Radical Social Work in the 1970s

The radical social work movement of the 1970s and early 1980s presents an interesting paradox for contemporary social workers. On the one hand, as noted above, radical social work has never been the dominant tradition within social work. On the other hand, as Powell correctly observes, 'radical social work has exercised an influence over social work's epistemology totally out of proportion to its minority status' (Powell, 2001: 68). One reason for this, as Powell notes, is that radical social work links a structural analysis of clients' problems to an ethical imperative to act, a combination that has proved attractive over the past three decades to social workers who feel that a concern for social justice should be a central part of social work. Second, in spite of (or perhaps because of) its minority status, radical social work became a favourite whipping boy of the New Right in the late 1970s and early 1980s, a useful vehicle for attacking the social work profession as a whole (see for example Brewer and Lait, 1980). A discourse of failure in relation to child protection was frequently linked to the alleged influence of radical ideas – initially Marxism, then feminism and latterly 'political correctness' in general (Philpot, 1999). In their attacks on anti-racist and anti-oppressive practice, a frequent refrain from politicians during much of the 1980s and 1990s was that social workers should be less concerned with such 'political correctness' and needed to acquire more 'commonsense'. For one Conservative Health Secretary in the mid-1990s, this involved the recruitment of more 'street-wise grannies' as social workers, while the first Health Minister (a consultant neurologist by profession) in the newly formed Scottish Executive opined that

> Social work services are not about redressing the major injustices in our world. Their remit is not to battle with the major forces that drive social exclusion. It is to promote social inclusion for each individual within their circumstances. (Sam Galbraith, cited in *Community Care*, 22 May 2000)

The ways in which radical social work actually impacted on social work practice will be considered later in this chapter. First, though, it is necessary to consider the origins and main themes of 1970s radical social work.

Radical Social Work: Origins, Politics and Main Themes

As I have argued in this chapter, since its origins in the nineteenth century, social work has always contained a potential for radicalism which has, from time to time, been realised in theories and forms of practice which have challenged the dominant methodologies. It is, however, in the 1970s, that radical social work, as a conscious and explicit approach to theory and practice really makes its appearance, both internationally and in Britain. Three main factors contributed to its emergence at this time:

First, in Britain in particular there was a growing realisation that the combination of the long post-war boom and the Welfare State had failed to eradicate fundamental problems of poverty and homelessness. As we saw in Chapter 2, Britain in the 1950s and early 1960s had been dominated by a consensus politics which assumed that, as a result of the above two factors, poverty would soon be a thing of the past. Problems that did remain were seen not as structural but rather as reflecting the defects of individual, families or communities (hence the centrality of the notion of 'the problem family' within social work during this period). That comfortable view was shattered, however, by the 'rediscovery of poverty' in many areas of the country by researchers such as Peter Townsend in the 1960s. In addition, powerful television documentaries such as Ken Loach's *Cathy Come Home* in 1966 shocked a nation into an awareness that homelessness, like poverty, was far from having disappeared, and led directly to the creation of the charity Shelter. In this sense, as Powell notes, what was new about the radical social work that was emerging, in contrast to earlier periods of social work radicalism, was its context:

> A welfare state had been created and social citizenship established. Radical social work contested the achievement of the welfare state and contested its flaws. (Powell, 2001: 69–70)

The re-emergence of economic crisis on a world scale in the early 1970s raised these problems to a qualitatively new level. In Britain, as we saw in Chapter 2, that crisis led to the return of mass unemployment by the late 1970s on a scale not seen since the 1930s. In this context of widespread poverty which clearly could not be blamed on individual failings, a social work practice which, as client research in the late 1960s had shown, persisted in employing concepts drawn from a bowdlerised psychoanalysis, was self-evidently less than relevant to the needs of clients, particularly their material needs.

A second factor fuelling social work's radical turn was the re-emergence of social revolt and rebellion at the end of the 1960's and 1970s on a scale not seen since the period following the First World War. Within this period the key year was 1968. As one historian of the events of that year has commented:

> What was unique about 1968 was that people were rebelling over disparate issues, and had in common only that desire to rebel, ideas about how to do it, a sense of alienation from the established order, and a profound distaste for authoritarianism in any form. Where there was communism they rebelled against communism, where there was capitalism, they turned against that. (Kurlansky, 2004: *xvii*)

The four main factors fuelling that rebellion, he suggests, were the example of the civil rights movement in the USA, a generation that felt completely alienated from consumer society, a universally unpopular war in Vietnam and the impact of television.

That movement and the feeling that 'everything was possible' sparked off a much more profound questioning of every aspect of human life, including such diverse issues as the place of women in society, the meaning of madness and our understanding of sexuality. It gave rise to both the women's liberation movement and the gay movement, while in Britain and France in particular, it linked with economic grievances to give rise to the biggest waves of workers' struggles seen in Europe since the 1920s and 1930s (Harman, 1988). In terms of social work, it led to a search for new ways of relating to clients based on human solidarity, more critical understandings of the family as an institution and a recognition of the value of collective approaches.

The crisis, both economic and ideological, of the Welfare State on the one hand and the re-emergence of collective protest on the other gave rise to the third factor fuelling the emergence of a new, radical social work: the entry into social work in the late 1960s and early 1970s of young people, often sociology graduates, for whom working in the new, generic social work departments appeared to offer a way of making a living that was to some degree compatible with their social and political ideals. A study by Pearson in the early 1970s found that

> The dominant impulse which brought them into the job was a rebellion against a life which they feared, otherwise, would waste their own human selves; they were runaways from commercialism, the 'rat race' and what they would describe as 'boredom'. (Pearson, 1974: 139)

In common with most social movements, the radical social work movement which developed in Britain during the 1970s did not possess a single coherent ideology but rather was made up of a number of different strands, sometimes overlapping, sometimes contradictory. In their history of radical social work in Britain, two former movement activists, Langan and Lee, suggest the existence of three distinct political currents within it (1989: 13–15). The first of these was a *revolutionary* current, which emphasised both the controlling aspects of social work and also the need for structural social change. These ideas were often expressed through the magazine *Case Con*, which argued for rank and file activism, the encouragement of democracy within the workplace and the union, and the development of closer links between workers and clients on the basis of common class interests (Simpkin, 1983; Langan, 2002: 212–13). A second strand, which Langan and Lee describe as *reformist*, placed more stress on defending the gains of the Welfare State and on developing strategies for working within it, while also emphasising work within the official structures of the Labour Party and the Trade Union Movement on the other. Third, there was what they call the *prefigurative* approach, influenced, they suggest by feminism and the slogan 'the personal is political.' Overlapping with this prefigurative approach was a libertarian or hippy strand, influenced by ideas of the 'counter culture' (Roszak, 1995). Pearson, in his critique of radical social work, probably exaggerates the importance of this libertarian strand, at times seeming to suggest that it was a dominant current within radical social work. In relation to the rising unemployment of the 1970s, for example, he writes that 'unemployment was not merely ignored within these [i.e. radical social work] discourses, it was actively promoted as a "progressive" and "liberating" lifestyle' (Pearson, 1989: 21). Given that some leading supporters of *Case Con* were actively involved in campaigns such as the National Right to Work Campaign which sought to challenge growing unemployment, this seems a rather skewed assessment.

As well as these differences, however, Langan and Lee also identify a number of themes which were common to most strands of radical social work in the 1970s (1989: 4–5). First, and most important, was the recognition that most of the problems which clients experienced were the product not of their personal failings or inadequacies but rather were the consequences of living in a society riven by inequality, oppression and class division. As Bailey and Brake put it in the introduction to their edited collection:

> Radical social work, we feel, is essentially understanding the position of the oppressed in the context of the social and economic structure they live in. (Bailey and Brake, 1975: 9)

The failure of social workers to address the material problems faced by their clients or more generally, to understand their clients' problems in the context of the poor communities in which they lived had been one of the key findings of *The Client Speaks* (Mayer and Timms, 1970). There were two consequences of that failure: First, it meant that material and financial problems were left unaddressed; second, it meant that problems of poverty were often interpreted as individual failings (an inability to budget, for example) or as reflecting underlying psychological problems. Not surprisingly, then, an emphasis on the structural roots of poverty – on *class* – coupled with the development of strategies aimed at alleviating that poverty, was a central theme of radical social work.

A second theme was the critique of casework. Casework was seen primarily as a means of individualising what were essentially collective problems. At best, therefore, it was ineffective; at worst, it was pathologising, since it encouraged clients to see themselves as personally responsible for the problems they were experiencing, rather than recognising that these problems were often the product of wider social and economic processes. In that sense, it was an ideological 'con'.

Third, there was the encouragement of collective approaches. In fact, the 'rediscovery' of community work as part of social work reflected a wider recognition of the limitations of individual work, shared by proponents of what were variously known as systems, ecological or unitary approaches (Pincus and Minahan, 1973; Specht and Vickery, 1976). The difference between the two approaches, however, lay in the goals for which community work approaches were employed. While systems theorists were primarily concerned with community work as a technique for restoring equilibrium between essentially harmonious social systems, radical social workers, drawing both on Marxist traditions and on the writing of community activists like Saul Alinsky (1973), saw community action (also the title of a long-running magazine aimed at community workers) as means both of promoting political change and of securing new resources in poor communities.

Fourth, there was the critique of professionalism. The basis of that critique was succinctly summed up in the *Case Con Manifesto* as follows:

> 'Professionalism' firstly implies the acquisition of a specialism – knowledge and skills not possessed by untrained workers. This isolates the social worker from the population at large. Secondly, social workers come to see themselves as part of an accepted specialist group on a par with doctors and lawyers. Third, it encourages the introduction of businesslike career structures, where 'correct' and 'professional' behaviour (such as 'detachment' and 'controlled emotional involvement') are rewarded with advancement. (Bailey and Brake, 1975: 145)

Two main consequences flowed from this critique of professionalism: First, it suggested a different kind of relationship with clients, one which emphasised the need to reduce worker–client power differentials on the one hand and the value of clients' knowledge and experience on the other. In that sense, it can be seen as a precursor to democratic models of user involvement which developed (particularly within the voluntary sector) in the 1990s (Beresford and Croft, 1995). Second, it eschewed the need for professional organisation in the form, for example, of the British Association of Social Workers (BASW), arguing that such organisations both encouraged elitism and replaced a focus on achieving social change and social justice in alliance with clients and other workers with a narrow concern for the promotion of professional interests. Instead, social workers should see themselves primarily as *workers*, whose primary form of organisation was the trade union. The astonishing growth of white-collar trade unionism in the 1970s (not least amongst social workers) and the failure of BASW in the UK even to recruit more than a relatively small percentage of the social work workforce shows that it was an argument that had a resonance well beyond the ranks of radical social workers (Simpkin, 1983; Payne, 2002).

Finally, the dominant analysis within the movement was a *socialist* analysis. For Bailey and Brake, for example,

> A socialist perspective is, for us, the most human approach for social workers. (Bailey and Brake, 1975: 9)

While there were very different views within the movement as to what socialism actually meant (with some writers viewing the erstwhile Soviet Union and its Eastern European satellites as socialist, and others seeing them as a different form of class-society) in practice, a socialist perspective meant seeing *class* as the central divide within society.

A common criticism of radical social work, both in its heyday and subsequently, has concerned the inability of its proponents to develop a radical practice on the basis of the above ideas. It is, allegedly, a theory in search of a practice. Even sympathetic writers such as Mullaly have argued that prior to the 1990s, radical social work was 'long on analysis but short on practice (1997: 106). It is a criticism, however, which Langan and Lee (along with commentators such as Powell, 2001: 85) reject:

> For the most part the critics of radical social work have ignored the extent to which radical social workers *are* steeped in practice. Many have been attracted to radical theory because they found conventional theory *inappropriate* for practice in the real world. Too often such theory is removed from reality, denying for example the impact of racism or the extent to which government legislation, particularly in the sphere of income maintenance, is making social workers agents of punitive and repressive policies. (1989: 7)

Where radical social work *did* fall down, they argue (as do many other critics) was in its failure to engage with the range of oppressions experienced both by social work clients and also by practitioners:

> Some of the absences in the early work are immediately apparent. There was little analysis of the role of women as the large majority of both social work clients and practitioners. Consideration of racism or of forms of anti-racist practice was minimal; there was no discussion about how to practise with the unemployed; older people and the non-able bodied were ignored. (1989: 5)

Conclusion: Evaluating Radical Social Work

The legacy of radical social work is a mixed one. As a specific approach to social work, it has been marginalised both within social work education and within social work practice for several decades, initially as a consequence of the shift in the political climate in British politics in the 1980s, then by the marketisation of social work initiated by the NHS and Community Care Act in the 1990s. Radical social work of course was not the only victim of this shift. Associated approaches such as community work, and even systems approaches, also suffered. It has meant, however, that for most of this period, radical social work, insofar as it has been discussed at all, has been seen as being of mainly historical interest.

Yet despite that marginalisation, the legacy of radical social work has continued to be felt in a number of different ways. First, its core ideas, in particular the notion of 'understanding the position of the oppressed in the context of the social and economic structure they live in' informed the development of anti-oppressive practice through the 1980s and 1990s (Dalrymple and Burke, 1995; Dominelli, 2002). Second, its call for a much more equal relationship between workers and clients, based both on a recognition of shared interests and also a valuing of the client's experience, prefigured the development of user involvement a decade later. Third, its emphasis on collective approaches, while less and less heeded within mainstream social work, was reflected in the growth of movements of service users in the 1980s, particularly the disability movement and the mental health users' movement (albeit largely without professional social work involvement). Fourth, while radical social work largely fell off the agenda in Britain, it continued to be developed as a living tradition elsewhere, notably in Canada and Australia. In these respects, radical social work has continued to make its influence felt. As Powell observes:

> Premature obituary notices have been written about radical social work. Its demise is unlikely. Radical social work is an authentic part of the social work tradition. It survives because it adapts and mutates. (2001: 87)

The means by which radical social work adapts and mutates form the subject of Chapters 7 and 8, the next two chapters. The Chapter 8 will explore the ways in which growing resistance to the values and practices of neo-liberalism, both inside social work and in the wider world, are creating new possibilities for resistance. For some social work writers, however, the re-evaluation of the radical tradition has led to the development of a 'critical social work practice' which is seen as encapsulating the best elements of radical social work while overcoming its perceived weaknesses, in particular an alleged overemphasis on class and a failure to adequately theorise and address issues of oppression. In Chapter 8 we shall explore the extent to which such critical social work perspectives – and more particularly, the embrace by some writers of postmodernism as a theoretical framework – offer a firmer basis for the development of a new, emancipatory practice in the twenty-first century.

7

Critical Social Work: Issues and Debates

Introduction: From Radical Social Work
to Critical Social Work

The period since the mid-1990s has seen the emergence of a body of social work writing usually referred to as *critical social work*, which some have seen as indicating the 'resurgence of radicalism' (Payne, 2005: 233). The term tends to be employed both in a broad and in a narrow sense. The broad sense is evident in Healy's definition of critical social work as including:

> Marxist social work; radical social work; structural social work; feminist social work; anti-racist social work; and anti-oppressive and anti-discriminatory social work. (Healy, 2005: 173)

What these different positions have in common, she argues, is an intellectual debt to 'the critical social science paradigm', with this term, too, meaning something wider than is sometimes the case in sociological discussions, where it usually refers to the body of Marxist, or Marxist-influenced, thought associated with the Frankfurt School of Adorno, Marcuse and Habermas (Jay, 1996). For Healy, by contrast, what defines critical social work is that it is

> concerned with the analysis and transformation of power relations at every level of social work practice. (Healy, 2005: 172)

She identifies the following four presuppositions/prescriptions as key elements of the critical social science paradigm:

(i)   'Macro-social structures shape social relations at every level of social life';
(ii) 'The world is divided between haves and have-nots and that the interests of these groups are opposed and irreconcilable';
(iii) 'The oppressed are complicit in their oppression';
(iv) 'Its emphasis [is] on empowering oppressed people to act, collectively, to achieve social change' (Healy, 2005: 173–4).

The continuities here with the earlier radical traditions are obvious, even if some of the key terms (e.g. 'haves' and 'have-nots') occasionally have a rather different meaning.

In contrast, in its narrow definition, what distinguishes critical social work from earlier radical or Marxist traditions is the incorporation of themes and concepts drawn from postmodernism and post-structuralism, philosophies with very different understandings of the nature of social division and the possibility (or even desirability) of social change. In important respects, both are founded on a sharp break with the critical social science paradigm to which Healy refers (Callinicos, 1989).

In her book on postmodern critical social work perspectives, Fook suggests that this approach is

> primarily concerned with practising in ways which further a society without domination, exploitation and oppression. It will focus both on how structures dominate, but also on how people construct and are constructed by changing social structures and relations, recognising that there may be multiple and diverse constructions in ostensibly similar situations. Such an understanding of social relations and structures can be used to disrupt dominant understandings and structures, and as a basis for changing these so that they are more inclusive of different interest groups. (Fook, 2002: 18)

There is, in fact, very little in this definition with which a Marxist social worker would disagree, whether it be the goal of 'a society without domination, exploitation and oppression' or the issue of how people construct their worlds, a central concern of Marxists from Marx himself (most notably in *The German Ideology* of 1845) through to Antonio Gramsci with his concept of *contradictory consciousness* (Gramsci, 1978). That said, later in this chapter I want to suggest that the implications of postmodernism for an emancipatory social work are more far-reaching, and less positive, than the above definition suggests.

As Davis and Garrett have observed (2004: 16), within the UK, social work's 'postmodern turn' has had little impact on practice and has been the subject of a number of critiques (Peile and McCouat, 1997; Smith and White, 1997; Ferguson and Lavalette, 1999; Williams, 1999; Dominelli, 2002). Elsewhere, however, postmodernism has become a key component of critical social work, particularly in the Australian literature, where a strong radical tradition had existed in the 1970s and 1980s (see for example Pease and Fook, 1999; Healy, 2000; 2005; Fook, 2002; Allan, Pease and Briskman, 2003). In Canada too, postmodernism appears to have made some inroads, with Peter Leonard, a leading figure in British radical social work in the 1970s and co-author of *Social Work Under Capitalism: A Marxist Approach* (Corrigan and Leonard, 1978), arguing that 'postmodernism provides a now essential ingredient in a revitalised Marxism' (Leonard, 1997: xiii). Given the international significance of this literature, the question of the extent to which postmodernism can provide a basis for an emancipatory practice clearly merits further discussion. Before that, however, I will briefly consider the movement from radical social work to critical social work (in the broad sense) which took place during the 1980s and 1990s, and the ways in which some understandings of oppression and difference which developed during this period contributed to the later emergence of postmodern social work.

Theorising Oppression

Perhaps the most frequent criticism of the radical social work tradition of the 1970s was its failure to engage sufficiently with the oppressions experienced by many social work clients, including women, black people and disabled people (Healy, 2005: 176–7). In their review of the tradition at the end of the 1980s, Langan and Lee themselves note that

> [s]ome of the absences in the early work are immediately apparent. There was little analysis of the role of women as the large majority of both social work clients and practitioners. Considerations of racism or of forms of anti-racist practice was minimal; there was no discussion about how to practice with the unemployed, older people and the non-able bodied were ignored. (1989: 5)

In contrast, during the 1980s, the oppression experienced by a range of different groups of people, and the struggle against these oppressions, became the central focus not only of critical social work theory and practice but of the political left more generally, involving what one writer described as a 'retreat from class' (Meiksins Wood, 1986). In Britain, and in other parts of the English-speaking world, the dominant critical perspectives within social work education and training in this period were feminism (Dominelli and McLeod, 1989; Hanmer and Statham, 1999), anti-racism (Dominelli, 1997) and anti-discriminatory/anti-oppressive practice (Dalrymple and Burke, 1995; Dominelli, 2003; Thompson, 2003).

Positively, that increased emphasis on oppression within social work has led to a heightened awareness on the part of social workers of the nature of the oppressions experienced not only by women and black people but also by people with disabilities, mental health problems and older people. One factor fuelling that awareness in the area of adult care was the emergence in the 1980s of the 'new social welfare movements' (Williams, 1992), which we discussed in Chapter 5, movements which have made a significant contribution to social work theory and practice. In addition, with the inclusion of anti-discriminatory and anti-oppressive practice within the social work curriculum in Britain, the early 1990s marked a further break with earlier pathologising perspectives (one reason why Conservative Governments throughout the 1990s continually sought to dilute or eradicate them – Dominelli, 2002).

In three respects, however, the direction taken by anti-oppressive practice in the 1990s was more problematic. First, there was the impact of paradigm shift, noted by Barrett and Phillips in their discussion of women's oppression, away from 1970s notions of oppression as rooted in social structures towards an emphasis on oppression as *identity* rooted in *difference* (Barrett and Phillips, 1992). Williams, while critical of aspects of this earlier paradigm, notes that it emphasised commonality and provided a basis for joint, collective action, not only between women and men but also between different groups of women (Williams, 1996: 65–7). In contrast, the 1990s emphasis on a politics of identity led to a fragmentation which often mirrored the fragmentation promoted by neo-liberal policies. As an example, consider Mullaly's discussion of oppression in his influential *Structural Social Work* (1997, 2nd edn). Here, he suggests that

> [w]omen are oppressed (by men) as women. Men are not oppressed as men. Non-whites are oppressed (by Whites) as non-Whites. Whites are not oppressed as Whites. Gay and lesbian persons are oppressed (by heterosexuals) as gay and lesbian persons. Heterosexuals are not oppressed as heterosexuals. (1997: 139)

He goes on to pose the question:

> Given that oppression is perpetrated by and perpetuated by dominant groups and is systematic and continuous in its application, a logical question is: why does it occur? The simple and correct answer is that oppression occurs because it benefits the dominant group. (1997: 139)

Let us begin by making three observations about this analysis of oppression. First, and despite the title of the book, structures appear to have vanished. The State does not make an appearance, nor does any ruling class. Rather, it is individuals, or groups of individuals, who oppress other individuals. It is not clear how the role of the State in oppressing asylum seekers, for example, or in the oppression of lone parents, would be covered by this analysis.

Second, if the analysis is correct, then any collective action would appear to be ruled out in advance – what advantage could there possibly be in forming alliances with your oppressors? In addition, since most people in one way or another are implicated in oppression (whether as Whites, straights, young people, middle-class people or whatever), then at best a very narrow form of 'identity' or pressure group politics would appear to be all that remains. In fact, as Smith notes in her critique of identity politics:

> Oppressions overlap, so that many people face more than one different form of oppression. Only in the world of abstraction can autonomous 'criss-crossing' antagonisms be fought separately. (Smith, 1994: 35)

Third, the analysis provides no basis for distinguishing between different forms of oppression; in a much-used phrase, there is 'no hierarchy of oppressions'. Insofar as this means that social workers need to challenge *all* forms of oppression, then it is unproblematic. Cutting oppression loose, however, from its roots in capitalism means that it becomes, in effect, subjectively defined. The result is, as Smith notes, that

> [t]his approach can and does result in trivialising genuine human suffering – by lumping it together with all in society who define themselves 'oppressed' – such as middle-class consumers or anti-authoritarian or middle-class youth – whose complaints may be valid but who hardly constitute specific groups within society. (1994: 28–9)

One group whose suffering has certainly been trivialised within social work as a consequence of such analyses of oppression is precisely that section of the working-class poor whose members are the biggest consumers of social work services. As Beresford and Croft have noted, by the early 1990s the emphasis on 'new social movements' throughout the previous decade had 'resulted in an over-rapid retreat from class analysis and class politics and the possibilities these offer for united action' (Cited in Cooke, 1996: 15). More recently, the political theorist Nancy Fraser has noted the ways in which an emphasis on identity has led to a devaluing of issues of poverty and inequality and has argued for a return to a 'politics of redistribution' (Fraser, 1995; 2000).

Despite these weaknesses, however, in practice many adherents of critical social work (in the broad sense) still sought to overcome this fragmentation and to make the links between oppression and material inequality. The extent to which postmodern critical social work is capable of making such linkages is much less clear and will be the subject of the remainder of this chapter.

What is Postmodernism?

Postmodernism is essentially a 'contrast' concept; it takes its meaning as much from what it claims to supersede or replace as from the positive elements of its definition (Kumar, 1995). Any discussion of postmodernism, therefore, has to start with a brief discussion of modernism and its related concept, modernity. Like postmodernism, modernism is subject to many, wide-ranging definitions. In his definitive study, the late Marshal Berman made a useful distinction between three key terms associated with modernism: First, *modernisation*, which refers to the economic, social and technological developments which emerged alongside capitalist society. Second, *modernism*, in the form of experimental movements in the arts from the futurists at the beginning of the twentieth century through to various tendencies in modern art in the 1960s. Finally, Berman refers to *modernity* as the radically transformed character of life under capitalism which began as a philosophical challenge (the Enlightenment) to traditionalism in the eighteenth century but reached its zenith in the major European and American cities of the late nineteenth and early twentieth centuries (Berman, 1982; 1999).

The major changes proclaimed by postmodernism mirror these three areas. In relation to economic and social development, adherents of postmodernism argue that capitalism has undergone a fundamental change, in one version from 'organised' to 'disorganised' capitalism (Lash and Urry, 1987), in another from a *Fordist* society, based on mass production involving the standardisation of products, Taylorist 'scientific management' of labour and assembly-line techniques, to *post-Fordism*, based on small-scale 'niche' production, the use of new computer-based technologies and with design and 'branding' a major selling-point (Burrows and Loader, 1994).

In relation to the second claim, postmodern art claims to have broken with modernist art movements and to be based on notions of eclecticism, pluralism and pastiche, the mixing of radically different elements and styles from different historical periods and different cultural traditions. As an example, postmodernists point to 1980s architecture, which often drew on old and new types of glass and brick, based around styles of architecture often centuries apart.

It is, however, for the philosophical challenge which it poses to modernism that postmodernism is most notorious. The nature of that challenge is summed up by one of postmodernism's leading thinkers:

> I define postmodern as incredulity toward metanarratives…. The narrative function is losing…its great hero, its great dangers, its great voyages, its great goal. It is being dispersed in clouds of narrative language elements….
>
> Thus the society of the future falls…within the province of a…pragmatics of language particles. There are many different language games – a heterogeneity of elements. They only give rise to institutions in patches – local determinism.
>
> The decision-makers, however, attempt to manage these clouds of sociality according to input/output matrices. (Lyotard, 1984: xxiv)

'Incredulity towards metanarratives' is the central tenet of postmodernism. 'Metanarratives' are attempts to make sense of the world as an interconnected whole or *totality*. Examples would include Marxism and feminism. For Lyotard, Baudrillard and followers, such attempts are misplaced for two reasons. First, they are based on the modernist or Enlightenment assumption that it is possible to discover objective 'scientific' truth about the world in which we live. Following post-structuralist thinkers like Foucault and Derrida, however, postmodernists argue that there is no 'objective reality' outside of language to be discovered; only language games, each presenting their own version of 'truth' – there is no Truth with a capital 'T'. Postmodernism, then, is an extreme form of *social constructionism* (Burr, 2003) or *anti-realism*, in which there are only different social constructions or local narratives, each one as valid as the other.

A second reason for rejecting metanarratives, postmodernists argue, is that the notion of a single Truth usually involves the suppression of other 'truths'. Metanarratives, in other words, lead to oppression and totalitarianism. The conclusion is that attempts to make sense of the world as an interconnected whole are not only misguided but dangerous. Instead, we should recognise that there are many voices or narratives, all with equal validity, and celebrate this diversity (including uncovering these voices which have previously been suppressed by dominant narratives).

The attractions of this perspective for a radical social work and a critical social policy are not hard to see. The history of welfare is a history of the suppression of the voices of service users and of their oppression by services geared to containment and control rather than to meeting human need, even when conducted in the language of care and concern. One need only think, for example, of the ways in which biomedical under-standings of mental ill-health have usually involved the suppression of service users' perspectives and experience (Rogers, Pilgrim and Lacey, 1993; Pilgrim and Rogers, 2003). Later in this chapter, the extent to which postmodernism can provide a firm theoretical basis for challenging such oppression will be considered in detail. First, however, it is necessary to consider some of the more general objections that have been made to postmodern theorising. These may be grouped under three headings: historical/sociological; philosophical; and ethical/political.

Historical/Sociological Objections

As a contrast concept, postmodernism implies that a particular historical period – modernity – is now over and has been replaced by a new period – postmodernity – characterised by different forms of social and industrial organisation, different forms of art and literature. These claims, however, have been challenged both on the grounds of their historical accuracy and also on their interpretation of the changes that have taken place. In terms of literature and art, for example, Callinicos has argued that many of the features supposedly associated with postmodern art – the juxtaposition of different styles, often from different historical periods, the use of montage, and so on – are in fact defining features of *modernism*, typical of the work of early twentieth-century writers such as Elliot and Joyce (Callinicos, 1989: 14–15). Similarly, in terms of the changes that have taken place in modes of production and industrial organisation, it has been argued that characterising capitalism in the late twentieth century as 'post-Fordist' both exaggerates the nature of the changes that have taken place (since capitalism has always been a dynamic system, constantly revolutionising its methods of production and distribution) and also underestimates the extent to which 'Fordist' modes of organisation have actually increased both socially (in terms of white-collar work, for example, in typing pools or call centres) and geographically (in countries such as Brazil, India and China) (Taylor-Gooby, 1997). No one would deny that real changes have taken place in the organisation of economic, social and cultural life in the late twentieth century. What many do dispute, however, is the way in which adherents of postmodernism interpret these changes (with one of the most important critics of postmodernism, Jurgen Habermas, preferring to describe the current period as 'High Modernity' – Habermas, 1987).

Philosophical Objections

A second set of objections concerns the anti-realist basis of postmodernism, the notion that there are no firm foundations to social life but only language games. While the philosophical basis of this view has been extensively challenged elsewhere (see for example Norris, 2000), in this chapter our main concern is with the implications of such a view. This aspect of postmodernism has been seen as particularly useful for social workers seeking to develop narrative approaches in their work with clients (Parton and O'Byrne, 2001; Fook, 2002; Healy, 2005). Yet as Pilgrim has noted in a paper critiquing the uses of postmodernism within family therapy (Pilgrim, 2000), postmodernists are far from being the only people to see the value of narrative approaches, or to recognise the socially constructed nature of the world in which we live, or to celebrate diversity. Moreover, the extreme social constructionism and anti-realism of postmodernism raises huge difficulties for those concerned with change, whether at an individual therapeutic level or at a wider structural level. He gives the example of a family where incestuous relationships were reported to have occurred down generations. While a *realist* approach would want to know whether the abuse had actually happened, in contrast, workers adopting *an anti-realist* stance would only be interested in the narratives which family members gave, since the 'truth' can never be established. Yet, as Pilgrim argues, clearly whether or not the abuse did actually happen would have important legal and therapeutic implications.

The point carries even greater weight in relation to social and structural issues.

In its denial of the existence of anything outside language, postmodernism denies us any access to these areas of life and consequently to the possibility of social change.

If there are only discourses and no material realities, then how can we hope, for example, to establish a relationship between class and mental ill-health, or between gender and depression, if the social 'facts' on which we rely to do so have no objective reality? As Pilgrim comments:

> postmodernism, by querying the relevance and reality of structures, actively resists the legitimacy of explanation. Postmodernism does not get its hands dirty with empirical investigations of reality. Instead it stands on the sidelines generating unending discourses about discourses. (Pilgrim, 2000: 13)

Ethical/Political Objections

The third set of objections to postmodernism relate to its ethical/political claims. The starting-point for postmodernism (and for post-structuralism)

Loan Receipt
Liverpool John Moores University
Library Services

Borrower Name: Leeks,Taran
Borrower ID: **********3114

Reclaiming social work :
31111012378491
Due Date: 26/01/2015 23:59

Radical social work today :
31111013487176
Due Date: 26/01/2015 23:59

Total Items: 2
05/01/2015 14:23

Please keep your receipt in case of
dispute.

is the rejection of the legacy of the Enlightenment. The Enlightenment refers to that group of mainly French and Scottish eighteenth-century intellectuals, including Adam Smith and David Hume in Scotland, Diderot and Voltaire in France and Kant in Germany, whose ideas represented a radical break with previous ways of understanding social and moral life (Broadie, 1997; Callinicos, 1999; Herman, 2001). Callinicos suggests that these thinkers had two decisive features in common: first, a model of rationality derived from Newtonian physics; second, an attempt to extend this scientific understanding to the whole of society (Callinicos, 1999: 15–16). In practice, this meant that human reason, not tradition or religion, should form the basis of society. In addition, it involved an attempt to understand society as an interconnected whole, often linked to optimistic notions of historical progress, in which one mode of society was replaced by another more advanced one (a notion most fully developed in the writings of the nineteenth-century German philosopher Hegel).

All of these assertions are rejected by postmodernists. First, rather than seeing history as progress, they follow another nineteenth-century German philosopher Friederich Nietzsche and his twentieth-century disciple Michel Foucault in seeing the 'will to power' as the driving force of human society. Notions of progress, evolution democracy, reason are so many shibboleths which simply mask the reality of oppression. Social life, like nature, is an endless struggle for domination. The conclusions which Nietzsche drew from this were essentially aristocratic, anti-democratic ones: only the strong individual, the 'Superman' could drag humanity forward. Following Nietzsche, Foucault similarly rejected Enlightenment notions of progress and much of his work, beginning with his history of madness, (Foucault, 1967) was concerned with uncovering and exploring the *discourses* (forms of power/knowledge) through which domination was exercised. Unlike Nietzsche, however, Foucault also saw the possibility for resistance: 'where there is power, there is resistance' (Foucault, 1981: 95). As power is everywhere, so too is resistance, hence the potential for localised struggles against oppression and domination (which in Foucault's own case meant supporting campaigns for prisoners' rights and for the rights of people with HIV/AIDS).

Second, whereas Enlightenment thinkers (and Hegel and Marx after them) sought to develop theories which made sense of society as an interconnected whole, postmodernists not only reject such 'grand narratives', such overarching explanations, both on epistemological grounds (as we saw above, there are only language games) but also because such attempts to 'privilege' one discourse over another (the discourse of class or gender, for example) are essentially attempts at domination which can only succeed at the price of the suppression of other discourses (such as blacks or gays). Therefore, all discourses are equally valid.

Space does not permit a full consideration of these postmodern claims but three brief points can be made: First, the recognition of the 'dark' side of modernity (or more specifically capitalism), including, for example, its failure to address the oppression of women and blacks, and its potential for oppression is far from new. The 'two-sided' nature of this new society – capitalism – and its potential to exploit and oppress as well as to create the material basis for freedom from hunger and want, was at the heart of Marx's critique of capitalism, while the oppressive potential of capitalist rationality informed both the writings of the German sociologist Max Weber and even more so, the writings of the Marxist Frankfurt School (Stirk, 2000) (Foucault expressed regrets in later life that he had not encountered the writings of the Frankfurt School much earlier). Rather than seeing the way out as involving the rejection of reason *per se*, however (which, incidentally, creates problems for postmodernism as a philosophy based on rational argument), other solutions are possible, including the notion of the 'radicalised Enlightenment', to be discussed in the final part of the chapter.

Second, if as Foucault and others argue, power is everywhere and if all discourses are equally valid, then the *ethical* basis for choosing one discourse over another, or for siding with the oppressed against the oppressor (as Foucault did) is not clear. In fact as another leading post-structuralist thinker Jacques Derrida admitted ' I try where I can to act politically while recognizing that such action remains incommensurate with my intellectual project of deconstruction' (Cited in Stirk, 2000: 59). In other words, the decision to challenge oppression or social inequality is a personal whim, no more and no less valid than the decision to participate in the oppression and exploitation of others. Some of the implications of this viewpoint for social work will be considered more fully in the next section.

Finally, the notion that any attempt to understand society as a whole (let alone bring about large-scale social change) will end in tyranny is also far from new. It is in essence the position of conservative thinkers from Edmund Burke in the 1790s through to the philosopher Karl Popper who, in his Cold War diatribes against Marx and Hegel, reached the conclusion that only 'piecemeal social engineering' was either possible or desirable, a conclusion that bears many similarities to the postmodern view that local struggles and local changes are the best we can hope for (Popper, 1945/2002). It is a profoundly conservative notion. If any attempt to bring about real change is likely to make things worse, then passivity and quietism become political virtues. In essence, we live in the best of all possible worlds.

Callinicos has argued that the historical roots of postmodernism's pessimism and passivity are to be found in the failure of the great social upheavals of the late 1960s to overthrow the bastions of capitalism and in the 'discovery' by erstwhile Marxists of the true extent of repression and brutality in so-called socialist regimes in places like Kampuchea and China. It is the resulting disillusionment, he argues, rather than any intrinsic intellectual coherence or worth, that has made postmodernism so attractive to many of those 'children of '68' who have given up any hope of bringing about large-scale societal change (Callinicos, 1989). As noted above, however, within social policy and social work postmodernism has also had an influence on people who clearly do want to fight oppression and injustice. The extent to which postmodernism can provide a firm, theoretical basis for that struggle will be the subject for the remainder of this chapter.

Postmodernism – Basis of Emancipatory Critique?

It is now common to distinguish between postmodernism as a means of 'characterising the present' (Browning, Halcli and Webster, 2000) – the 'postmodernisation thesis' – and what O'Brien and Penna refer to as 'social postmodernism' (O'Brien and Penna, 1998: 195), meaning postmodernism as the basis for a new politics. The main elements of this second aspect of postmodernism were outlined above. As we saw there, at the heart of such a postmodern politics is a 'radical perspectivism':

> It implies that since there is no factual ground on which to base theory and practice –in other words, there are no factual grounds on which to base true and false interpretations – then all knowledges of the world, including scientific and religious knowledges, are equally ungrounded interpretations of it. Poverty, disability, discrimination, it seems are not facts but interpretations and combating them is the expression of a value based on interpretation rather than a theory based on fact. (O'Brien and Penna, 1998: 196)

It is in the postmodern challenge to those 'knowledges' or 'grand narratives' that seek to make sense of the world as a totality – which in the field of welfare, tends to mean structuralist theories such as Marxism or feminism – that some writers have seen the possibility of a new 'emancipatory' politics of welfare (Leonard, 1997; Wilson, 1997; Pease and Fook, 1999).

The charge against these overarching theories in the sphere of welfare is twofold. First, it is argued, they are reductionist. In seeking to make sense of the whole, they 'flatten' difference and diversity, in the process reducing and distorting whole areas of social experience. In a critique of class-based explanations in sociology, for example, Bradley argues that

> The recognition that social inequalities and divisions could not be subsumed under one monolithic theory, that of class, led to a growing appreciation of the complexity of social differentiation in multi-cultural, post-colonial societies, where many sources of difference – class, gender, ethnicity, 'race', age, region, dis/ability, sexual orientation – intertwined to produce multi-faceted and intricate forms of social hierarchy. (Bradley, 2000: 478)

While in the first instance, this critique of Marxist approaches came in the 1980s from feminist and black nationalist writers wishing to stress the 'autonomy' of gender and 'race', it converged neatly with emerging postmodern perspectives which

> saw society in terms of a multitude of social groupings which formed around different potential sources of identity and had their own distinctive cultures, lifestyles and consumption patterns. (2000: 478)

A second criticism of the operation of 'grand narratives' in the area of social welfare is that they distort, deny and silence the experience of minorities and consequently, whatever the intentions of their adherents, they function as part of an apparatus of power and oppression which serves the interest of specific privileged groups. Those who wish to develop 'emancipatory practice' on the basis of postmodern perspectives, therefore, would see their role as being to 'give a voice' to those whose voices have historically been ignored or silenced within dominant discourses, including those discourses which portray themselves as discourses of emancipation. The link between such a politics and the wider theoretical premises of postmodernism is summarised by Leonard as follows:

> Because meaning is continually slipping away from us, there can be no essential, certain meanings, only different meanings emerging from different experiences, especially the experiences of those who have been excluded from discourses, whose voices and whose writing have been silenced. In the Western culture of modernity, this has meant especially the excluded voices of women, non-white populations, gays and lesbians and the working classes in general. (Leonard, 1997: 10–11)

The main implication of this approach for the formulation of a critical social work and social policy is an emphasis on 'particularism' as opposed to the 'false universalism' of the post-war Welfare State, with its assumption of the white, able-bodied heterosexual male as the norm, an assumption which in practice was used to deny the needs of certain groups, including women and black people. Thompson and Hoggett summarise the postmodernist case in the area of social policy as follows:

> [I]n the name of particularism, diversity and difference, such policy should not be formulated within a guiding framework that is universalist in character; it may even question the desirability of incorporating *any* significant element of universalism into social policy. (Thompson and Hoggett, 1996: 23)

That many groups in society, including people with disabilities and people with mental health problems, as well as working-class women and members of ethnic minorities, have experienced aspects of the operation of the Welfare State as disempowering and oppressive is well-documented. The extent to which a social work practice based on particularism and informed by postmodern perspectives would challenge that oppression, however, is much less clear. Three particular aspects of postmodern thought must give cause for serious doubt: its individualism; its rejection

Would particularism help MH SO's?

of structural explanations of poverty and inequality; and its moral relativism.

A Postmodern Critical Social Work?

First, let us consider individualism. In a sense the very idea of a postmodern *social* work is a contradiction since at the heart of postmodernism is a radical individualism. Postmodernism goes beyond identity politics in rejecting not only class as a basis of common interest and action but *all* bases of collective identity – whether gender, disability or 'race' – since they are all premised on a wider narrative about how the world works. One might assume that that would disqualify postmodernism from making any contribution to debates about social work and social policy. In fact postmodernism's individualism and emphasis on individual *Oh dear!* consumption make it quite compatible with social policies which are very far from being radical or emancipatory. As one writer sympathetic to postmodern perspectives has commented:

> In practical policy terms, postmodernism can be seen to fit all too well with a government that denies the existence of society and prioritises individual expenditure over public welfare. (Wilson, 1997: 349)

While Wilson is mainly referring to the social policies of the British Conservative Governments of the 1990s, her comments also have relevance for the policies of governments in Britain and elsewhere based on 'Third Way' notions. For as Jones and Novak note, under New Labour:

no collection

> As in contemporary theories of postmodernism, people are identified not by their collective experiences – as workers, as women or black people – but as individuals. It is not the same individualism as that of the new right, although it draws many parallels, not least with the 'active citizens' that fleetingly formed part of John Major's agenda in the early 1990s. The new right's individualism was of the sink or swim variety. New Labour's individualism is much more actively promoted. (Jones and Novak, 1999: 179)

In fact, core postmodernist themes – the celebration of 'ephemerality, fragmentation, discontinuity'; the rejection of structural explanations of poverty and inequality; adoration of all that is new and 'modern', coupled with an ironic disdain for 'old-fashioned' notions of commitment and solidarity – chime in very well with current 'Third Way' notions of welfare with their stress on the 'end of ideology'.

Second, consistent with the individualist emphasis noted above, there is the postmodern rejection of *structural* explanations of poverty and inequality. In contrast to Marxist approaches, which are primarily concerned with the ways in which one class (comprising a very small number of people) is able to use its economic, political and ideological power to exploit and oppress another class or classes (comprising a very large number of people), postmodern theorists and their post-structuralist predecessors like Foucault, see power as *omnipresent*, as everywhere (and one might argue, nowhere):

> When I think of the mechanics of power, I think of its capillary forms of existence, of the extent to which power seeps into the very grain of individuals, reaches right into their bodies, permeates their gestures, their position, what they say, how they learn to live and work with other people. (Foucault, quoted in Watson, 2000: 68)

As Watson correctly comments on this passage:

> Such a view stands in clear opposition to the notion that the state or capital as a concentrated site of power needs to be overthrown or dismantled for socialism or universal social justice to be achieved. (Watson, 2000: 68)

In fact, the implications for social work and social policy potentially go much further than a rejection of the revolutionary socialist case for the overthrow of capitalism. Postmodernism's view of power and resistance as essentially localised and located in the micro-relations between men and women, black and white, and so on is at best likely to lead to a focus on local issues, small-scale studies. Since large-scale societal transformation is neither possible nor desirable, the best that can be hoped for is reform at a local or individual level. Some writers (e.g. Healy, 2000) have seen this as a strength, rather than a weakness, of postmodern approaches and criticise radical social workers in the past for devaluing work with individual and local groups. There is no doubt that many radicals in the 1970s *were* dismissive of individual approaches, mainly because, as early consumer research in Britain had shown (Mayer and Timms, 1970) the dominant form on offer – psychosocial casework – did not appear to address the social and material needs of working-class clients. That said, not all radical social workers rejected individual work. As noted in Chapter 6, the previous chapter, in the introduction to their seminal collection, for example, Bailey and Brake, drawing on the ideas of Antonio Gramsci, argued that 'Our aim is not ... to eliminate casework, but to eliminate casework that supports ruling-class hegemony' (1975: 9). As well as in addressing material problems,

> a consideration of the personal sphere must also remain – hating one's gender role, loving the same gender, hating one's occupation, disliking one's parents, spouse of children is not personal inadequacy. The danger of hegemony is that it may result in psychological damage to those who oppose it. In this way casework may assist people to resist hegemony and develop pride instead of self-hatred. A framework of cultural diversity is more illuminating than an uncritical acceptance of the ideology of 'normal'. (1975: 10)

Moreover, most community workers (including myself) were often employed as *neighbourhood* workers, involved in precisely the kind of local issues that Healy talks about, including (in my own case) housing campaigns, anti-dampness campaigns and campaigns against cuts in local services. The weakness of postmodernism, however, is that it provides no practice or theoretical framework for making the links between such individual and local groupwork and wider structural processes. To use a contemporary example, it is impossible to understand or to effectively challenge the erosion of therapeutic relationships in social work of which contributors both to Jones' research in England and to the 21st Century Review of Social Work in Scotland, *Changing Lives*, complained without locating that erosion within the context of the marketisation of social work and the current dominance of care management approaches (Scottish Executive, 2006a). As Wilson has rightly noted:

> The unwillingness of the postmodernists to conceptualise structured power relations in a traditional way presents problems for those who work with or study disadvantaged groups. (Wilson, 1997)

In fact, there are indications that the influence of postmodern ideas in welfare thinking is already starting to have a negative impact in this area. In an early critique, Taylor-Gooby expressed the fear that a growth in influence of postmodern perspectives within social policy would lead to a neglect of issues concerning poverty and inequality:

> The implications for social policy are that an interest in postmodernism may cloak developments of considerable importance. Trends towards increased inequality in living standards, the privatisation of state welfare services and the stricter regulation of the lives of some of the poorest groups may fail to attract the appropriate attention if the key themes of policy are seen as difference, diversity and choice. (Taylor-Gooby, 1994: 403)

Since then, a number of writers have noted the paradox that at a time when the gap between rich and poor has been shown by numerous studies to be greater than it has ever been (and, as we saw in Chapter 2, in the UK context has continued to grow under a New Labour government), the lack of interest amongst social science academics in exploring class and material inequalities has never been greater (Bradley, 2000; Mooney, 2000). While it would be misleading to attribute the neglect of these issues solely to the growth of postmodernism, not least since this neglect goes back to the 1980s (Becker, 1997), it is nevertheless arguable that the Foucauldian emphasis on the 'the specific, the local and the particular' (Watson, 2000: 76) reinforces and legitimises that neglect (and in fact, the failure to address the material realities which shape the lives of service users is a striking feature of some of the literature seeking to develop a full-blown postmodern, or 'constructive', social work (Parton and O'Byrne, 2001).

Finally, there is postmodernism's oft-noted moral relativism. In a previous paper, we have considered some of the implications of that relativism for anti-oppressive social work practice (Ferguson and Lavalette, 1999). Suffice it to say that a metanarrative (for of course, as several critics have noted, postmodernism is itself a metanarrative) which refuses to 'privilege' any discourse over any other scarcely provides a firm foundation for a critical social work or social policy. As Crook has noted:

> When radical social theory loses its accountability, when it can no longer give reasons, something has gone very wrong. But this is precisely what happens to postmodern social theory, and it seems very appropriate to use the over-stretched term 'nihilism' as a label for this degeneration. The nihilism of postmodernism shows itself in two symptoms: an inability to specify mechanisms of change, and an inability to state why change is better than no change. (Crook, 1990: 59)

Conclusion: The Alternative to Particularism – the 'Radicalised Enlightenment'

In the light of the above discussion, it may seem strange that postmodernism should hold any attractions for critical social work or social policy theorists, particularly those committed to what Leonard has dubbed 'emancipatory welfare' (Leonard, 1997). It is nevertheless true that many of those who are drawn towards the ideas of post-structuralism and post-modernism see these ideas as *more* radical than the traditional alternative of Marxism. In explaining that attraction, two factors seem of particular significance. On the one hand, there is a widespread disillusionment with the version of Marxism associated with the Communist Parties internationally, reinforced by the collapse of what are usually (and, I would argue, misleadingly) referred to as the 'state socialist regimes' of the former Soviet Union and Eastern Europe. We have argued elsewhere that Stalinism in theory and practice, not least in its influential Althusserian incarnation, is the antithesis of the genuine Marxist tradition and, rather than repeat these arguments here, would refer readers to previous publications (Ferguson and Lavalette, 1999; Ferguson, Lavalette and Mooney, 2002). On the other hand, there has been a growing scepticism regarding the 'false universalism' of welfare policy, partly in response to the growth of movements such as the disability movement. It is this latter point which I shall briefly address here.

It is worth noting that the 'false universalism' not simply of the Welfare State but more generally of the Enlightenment, is not a new theme. As Callinicos has noted:

> Ever since Marx and Nietzsche in their different ways subjected the Enlightenment to critical scrutiny, the very ideas of universality and rationality have been under suspicion for secreting within themselves hidden particularisms …the universal

rights and happiness promised by the French and the American revolutions tacitly excluded, among others, slaves, the poor and women. (Callinicos, 1999: 310)

As he goes on to argue, there are really only two ways to respond to these limitations of the Enlightenment's promise of universal emancipation. One is to conclude that every universalism is a masked particularism and then decide which particularism (or coalition of particularisms) one prefers – the postmodern option. In terms of welfare policy, the dangers of such a strategy, particularly during a period of welfare retrenchment, are obvious. At best, it can allow governments, whose overriding concern is limiting welfare expenditure, to play off one group against another as they squabble over the limited resources on offer. At worst, it can contribute to a backlash against oppressed groups whose legitimate demands for affirmative action or positive discrimination can be portrayed as being at the expense of the basic welfare needs of the majority – one factor used in the undermining of the policies of left-wing Labour councils Britain in the 1980s and seen in recent attacks on 'political correctness' (Smith, 1994; Penketh, 2000).

Alternatively, Callinicos argues, one can respond to the failures of the Enlightenment project by seeking a *genuine* universality, a social and political order from which no one is excluded. A powerful plea for this latter position from the perspective of the disability movement is provided by Oliver and Barnes when they argue that

> Although versions of the good society vary, for us it is a world in which all human beings, regardless of impairment, age, gender, social class or minority ethnic status can co-exist as equal members of the community, secure in the knowledge that their needs will be met and that their views will be recognised and valued ... for us, disabled people have no choice but to attempt to build a better world because it is impossible to have a vision of inclusionary capitalism; we all need a world where impairment is valued and celebrated and all disabling barriers are eradicated. Such a world would be inclusionary for all. (Oliver and Barnes, 1998: 102)

In contrast to the pessimism of postmodernism, this view implies the possibility of successful collective action on the basis of opposition to neo-liberal versions of globalisation, a process and structure which, *pace* postmodernism, can be both understood and challenged. The nature of the challenge in the first decade of the twenty-first century, and its implications for a critical social work, will be considered in the Chapter 8.

8

Challenging the Consensus

Introduction: Neo-liberalism and Its Discontents

The year 2006 saw the publication of *After the Neo-Cons: America at the Crossroads* by politics professor and former US State Department official Francis Fukuyama (Fukuyama, 2006). *After the Neo-Cons* was a blistering critique of the foreign policies of the neo-conservatives, that group of politicians, advisers and academics around President George W. Bush who devised the Project for the New American Century which set out a rationale and strategy for US economic and military domination of the globe in the twenty-first century (Callinicos, 2003). What made the book significant was not so much its content (by 2007, the view that the US-led invasion and occupation of Iraq had been a huge foreign policy error, and had led to a humanitarian disaster of unimaginable proportions, was already a majority view in the USA, Britain and Iraq itself) but rather its author. Fukuyama's previous book, *The End of History and the Last Man* (1993), had been one of the most influential texts of the 1990s. There, echoing at a more sophisticated level the populist rhetoric of politicians like Margaret Thatcher, he had argued that, following the collapse of communism, no systemic alternative to liberal capitalism was possible. His work was hugely significant in providing an ideological underpinning to the 'Washington Consensus', the common-sense view of many governments in the 1990s that only measures such as privatisation of public services, deregulation, tax reform and fiscal discipline could produce vibrant, healthy economies. The real significance of *After the Neo-Cons*, therefore, was primarily symbolic. The fact that one of the leading neo-conservatives had turned against his erstwhile comrades was one indication amongst many, albeit a particularly striking one, that the neo-liberal and neo-conservative 'common sense' of the previous two decades was fragmenting. N Lib

In the first part of this chapter, I wish to consider two other challenges to neo-liberalism which have emerged in recent years and explore their implications for a new, engaged social work practice. First, I shall discuss the 'happiness' literature which has flourished in recent years and which offers a critique (of sorts) of some of aspects of neo-liberal society. To the extent that this new 'science' asserts that there may be more to life than

[handwritten: more to life . than consumerism]

consumerism, it can be seen as challenging one of the main assumptions of neo-liberal ideology (as well as sharing some affinities with social work values).

Second, there is the anti-capitalist (or global justice) movement, briefly discussed in Chapter 1, which emerged out of the demonstrations against the proceedings of the World Trade Organisation (WTO) in Seattle in 1999, survived the backlash against any form of dissent following the events of 9/11 in 2001 and went on to fuel the growth of a huge global movement against war and occupation in Iraq. In Chapter 6, I discussed some of the ways in which social movements in earlier periods have impacted on, and often radicalised, social work practice. Here, I shall consider how the social movements of our own time might similarly strengthen critical currents within contemporary social work.

These challenges to neo-liberal ideas and values also find a strong echo from *within* social work and, continuing the discussion begun in Chapter 3, the next part of the chapter will explore the ways in which the experience of working within 'neo-liberal social work' is creating dissatisfaction and dissent among wide layers of social workers. What is particularly significant about this dissatisfaction, I shall argue, is that, in contrast to the movement of the 1970s, it affects not just a small layer of 'radical' social workers (however one defines that term in the twenty-first century) but also many 'traditional' workers who feel that their values and notions of good practice are being undermined. Where that dissatisfaction is given a voice, as it has been in various forums in recent years, it becomes possible to glimpse both a different kind of social work and also the kind of collective organisation that can help make that alternative vision a reality. The final part of the chapter will look at how we might 'reclaim' social work from what it has become following two decades of neo-liberal policies, and develop forms of theory and practice which allow practitioners to make a positive difference to the lives of those with whom they work and the communities they inhabit.

Neo-liberalism and Its Discontents: 'The Science of Happiness'

The issue of happiness – what it is and how to get it – has become one of the dominant discourses of the first decade of the twenty-first century. A concern with happiness in itself is, of course, hardly new. The relationship between happiness and other valued social goals such as justice and freedom has been a central concern of philosophers since Aristotle onwards. Current discussions about happiness, however, differ in two important respects. First, there is the sheer scale of the current concern. Happiness in recent years has become an industry. At an international level, the industry has its own academic journal – the *Journal of Happiness Studies*. Over 3,000 articles have been published on the subject of happiness, and numerous websites have been set up, with Professor Martin Seligman's *Authentic Happiness* website probably the best known, claiming some 400,000 users (Seligman, 2002). Within the UK, the Centre for Confidence and Well-being was launched in Scotland in December 2004, with Seligman the keynote speaker at its founding conference, and with the aim of overcoming what its founder and CEO, psychologist Dr Carol Craig, has labelled 'the Scots' crisis of confidence' (Craig, 2003a). Finally, the past few years have seen an astonishing outpouring of books on the theme of happiness, with titles ranging from *Happiness: Lessons from a New Science* by Richard Layard, Professor of Economics at the LSE at one end of the spectrum to *Positively Happy: Cosmic Ways to Change Your Life* by the entertainer Noel Edmonds at the other.

A second factor distinguishing the current interest in happiness from that of earlier periods is the way in which particular notions of happiness are increasingly shaping government policy, particularly in the area of mental health. Thus, the Centre for Confidence and Well-being receives financial support from the Scottish Executive, while its first chairperson was also chairperson of the major 21st Century Review of Social Work in Scotland. It is, however, at the UK level that the impact of this new happiness discourse is most strongly felt. Here the key role has been played by a professor from the London School of Economics, Richard Layard, who is also a member of the House of Lords. In contrast to the other key figures involved in this movement, Layard is not a psychologist but is an economist. As well as being author of *Happiness: Lessons from a New Science* (Layard, 2005), he is also one of the authors of *The Depression Report* published in June 2006, the findings of which will be considered below (CEPMHPG, 2006).

So how is the current obsession with happiness to be explained? Clearly, it seems to suggest something about people's experience of the society they live in. For more than two decades, the promise of neo-liberalism has been that the 'trickle down' of wealth will result not only in a wealthier society but also a *better* society, in the sense of happier, more contented citizens (or consumers). The reality, however, seems to be very different. In the words of the leading British advocate of the 'science of happiness':

> There is a paradox at the heart of our lives. Most people want more income and strive for it. Yet as Western societies have got richer, their people have become no happier... But aren't our lives infinitely more comfortable? Indeed we have more food, more clothes, more cars, bigger houses, more central heating, more foreign holidays, a shorter working week, nicer work and, above all, better health. Yet we are not happier. Despite all the efforts of governments, teachers, doctors and businessmen, human happiness has not improved. (Layard, 2005: 3–4)

The popularity of this literature, and the growth of happiness industry more generally, suggests that this analysis strikes a chord with many people. Similarly some of the solutions which these writers propose – an emphasis

[handwritten annotation: meaning / less comparing.]

on meaning and purpose in life as opposed to an obsession with achievement or consumption; less comparing ourselves with others; the attainment of 'flow' (total involvement and loss of self in meaningful and creative activities), and (in some cases) a call for more equal societies – are also likely to find favour with those unhappy with their lives.

Moreover, some of these writers are not afraid to locate the roots of the current malaise in the 'greed is good', neo-liberal ethos which has prevailed since the 1980s.

Psychologist Oliver James, for example, in his best-selling book *Affluenza* (James, 2007) roots the problem in what he calls the 'Affluenza Virus', which he defines as:

> A set of values which increase our vulnerability to emotional distress. It entails placing a high value on acquiring money and possessions, looking good in the eyes of others and wanting to be famous. Just as having the HIV virus places you at risk of developing the physical disease of AIDS, infection with the Affluenza Virus increases your susceptibility to the commonest emotional distresses: depression, anxiety, substance abuse and personality disorder (like 'me, me, me' narcissism, febrile moods or confused identity). (James, 2007: vii)

To a greater extent than some of his co-thinkers in the Happiness Forum, formed in 2003, (James, 2007: 319), James pulls no punches in his critiques either of what he calls 'selfish capitalism', or of the values and lifestyles of leading New Labour Ministers.

The strength of the 'happiness' literature, then, lies in its description of the ways in which consumerist society not only does not lead to greater personal happiness for many but has resulted in unprecedented levels of mental ill-health. Its major weakness, however, lies in the individualism which underpins some of its most influential versions (such as Seligman's Positive Psychology – Seligman, 2002) and which makes it easily compatible with a neo-liberal emphasis on health and well-being as personal responsibility. Nowhere is this clearer than in the *Depression Report*, which is likely to have considerable influence on government mental health policy and whose arguments we shall now consider.

As mentioned above, the lead writer of *The Depression Report*, subtitled 'A new deal for depression and anxiety disorders' (CEPMHPG, 2006) was Richard Layard. The language of 'new deals' is not accidental. From 1997 to 2001 Layard was an Adviser to New Labour and one of the key architects of its New Deal and Welfare to Work Policies.

The Report's starting-point – that 'crippling depression and chronic anxiety are the biggest causes of misery in Britain today' – is one with which few would disagree. Quoting the Psychiatric Morbidity Survey, Layard and his colleagues note that one in six of us would be diagnosed as having depression or chronic anxiety disorder, which means that one family in three is currently affected.

However, while similar findings about the extent of depression almost thirty years ago led Brown and Harris to pose hard questions about the kind of society that gives rise to such levels of misery (Brown and Harris, 1978), such concerns do not appear to trouble the authors of this report. Instead, their second finding – the 'good news' as they call it – is that most of this misery is totally unnecessary and avoidable, since 'we now have evidence-based therapies that can lift at least half of those affected out of their depression or chronic fear' (2006: 1). Foremost amongst these evidence-based therapies is cognitive behaviour therapy (CBT).

This, they argue, is good news for two groups of people. Most obviously, it is good news for those who are currently experiencing mental distress. It is also, however, good news for a New Labour Government in the UK seeking to reduce spending on benefits for people with disabilities. For, the Report reminds us, as well as such mental ill-health being a waste of people's lives:

> It is also costing a lot of money. For depression and anxiety make it difficult or impossible to work, and drive people onto Incapacity Benefit. We now have half a million people on Incapacity Benefits because of mental illness – more than the total number of people receiving unemployment benefit. (2006: 1)

A key objective of the Report, therefore, is to find ways of reducing the number of people with mental health problems currently claiming Incapacity Benefit.

In order to achieve these objectives, the Report proposes the recruitment of 10,000 CBT therapists. Of these, 5,000, would be fully trained clinical psychologists, clearly envisaged as the elite troops of this new mental health service. Backing up these clinicians would be another 5,000 'psychological therapists', trained in CBT on a part-time basis over a year or two, and working under the supervision of the clinical psychologists. These psychological therapists would be mainly nurses, occupational therapists, counsellors and social workers. These would be trained and recruited over the next seven years, with the aim being that by 2013 there would be some 250 teams in place in England and Wales with around 40 therapists in each.

On the all-important question of costs, by 2013 the gross costs of the service would have reached about £600 million a year, with an additional annual training cost of around £50 million. However, the Report's authors suggest, these costs would be 'fully offset, of course, by rapid savings to the Department of Works and Pensions and HM Revenue and Customs' – presumably by removing hundreds of thousands of people from Incapacity Benefit.

Given current levels of mental distress in the UK, any proposal which seeks to improve and expand accessible services for those suffering in this way is to be welcomed, particularly when it involves an increase in the talking therapies which, as surveys over the years have shown, many service users find preferable to drug-based treatments (Rogers, Pilgrim and Lacey, 1993). However, the arguments of *The Depression Report*, and, by extension, of the 'science of happiness', are open to a number of objections, most of which relate to the role of ideas in creating happiness, unhappiness and mental distress.

Ideas play a central role in much of the happiness literature, whether it be Craig's assertion that the Scots' alleged lack of confidence is primarily 'an attitude problem' (Craig, 2003b) or Layard's embrace of cognitive behavioural approaches which see depression primarily as the product of faulty thinking, and of cognitive distortions (Nelson-Jones, 2000).

Challenging harmful or oppressive ideas, whether at an individual or a collective level, and whether in relation to mental health or other forms of oppression or discrimination is, of course, often a good thing to do. The Scottish Executive's *See Me* campaign, for example, which challenges stigmatising attitudes towards people with mental health problems, has helped shift attitudes towards mental ill-health in Scotland (www.seemescotland. org). The same is true of other similar campaigns which the Executive has sponsored in recent years, for example, against domestic violence and against racism.

Similarly, at an individual level, there is clear evidence that many people find counselling or therapeutic approaches which challenge negative beliefs or reframe thought patterns at an individual level, such as CBT, to be helpful (Cigno, 2002).

Several objections can be made, however, to the suggestion of Layard and his colleagues that, as an 'evidence-based' approach, CBT should become the primary, if not the sole, form of therapy on offer to those experiencing depression or anxiety.

First, there is the uncritical acceptance within much of the happiness literature of positivist notions of science, and of what constitutes evidence. The fact that CBT, like other behavioural approaches, lends itself more easily than other therapies to quantitative methods of evaluation is not the same as saying that is necessarily more effective. As we saw in the discussion of evidence-based practice in Chapter 3, randomised control trials are not the only, or even the most effective, way of measuring how helpful a particular therapy may be (Gray and MacDonald, 2006). Significantly, neither in *The Depression Report* nor in the happiness literature more generally is there any reference to the considerable body of mental health user research that has been created over the past decade which both critiques the medical model and shows what service users find helpful. On the contrary, within the work of Layard in particular, there appears to be an uncritical acceptance of the medical model of mental health.

Second, while there is research evidence to show that CBT can be effective for people with simple, uncomplicated, mild depression, there is less evidence for its effectiveness in helping people with more complicated or prolonged depression, including depression arising from early trauma – the sort of people who will often figure prominently in the caseloads of social workers, often with the label of 'personality disorder' (Ferguson, Barclay and Stalker, 2003; McPherson, Richardson and Leroux, 2003; Pidd, 2006).

For these people, other approaches will often be necessary, which in some cases might involve 'working through' earlier abusive experiences, in others, greater use of social networks and social supports. Different approaches, in other words, are likely to work for different people. In this respect, there is a certain irony in the fact that a government which lambasts a 'one size fits all' approach in other areas of health and social care should be seriously considering the adoption of such an approach in the field of mental health policy.

Third, despite the overriding role which Layard and the other 'science of happiness' theorists give to *ideas* in the creation of mental ill-health, there is curiously little interest in any of these texts in where these supposedly irrational ideas come from, or why people persist in holding onto them (a partial exception being Craig who locates what she sees as the Scots' lack of confidence within a dependency culture bred by a long-standing collectivist culture). Yet as the nineteenth-century Italian Marxist Antonio Labriola rather eloquently put it 'Ideas do not fall from heaven, and nothing comes to us as in a dream' (www.marxists.org/archive/labriola/works/al01.htm). In other words, if people persist in holding damaging or irrational ideas that adversely affect their mental health – the belief for example that they are inferior, or even worthless, human beings – then surely we should be looking to see where these ideas come from, and why they seem so powerful?

The most important objection to the 'science of happiness', however, is that it systematically ignores the entire question of social inequality. Despite frequent references to 'evidence-based' practice, there is no discussion anywhere within *The Depression Report* of one of the most powerful bodies of evidence in any field of social science research anywhere: namely, the tight link between inequality and every type of mental ill-health (Pilgrim and Rogers, 2002). In this respect it is interesting to contrast the arguments of Layard with the analysis of depression developed by Brown and Harris in their classic text of the late 1970s (Brown and Harris, 1978). In common with the happiness theorists, they too argued that in the development of depression 'it is change in *thought* about the world that is crucial' (1978: 273). Unlike the Happiness theorists, however, they sought to locate that change in thought in a complex and holistic model which acknowledged the role of both past and present experience, particularly class experience, as well as social supports and networks in shaping a mindset which, they argue, can protect against, or predispose towards depression. That model helped explain their finding that working-class women were four times more likely to develop depression than middle-class women.

The silence of Layard and his co-thinkers on issues of inequality is a major cause for concern, given the intellectual and political climate in which they are being proposed and the uses to which they are likely to be put. For whether it be Layard's insistence that CBT can reduce by half the number of people with mental health problems on Incapacity Benefit, or Craig's view that the roots of Scotland's problems lie in its dependency culture, the key themes of the science of happiness fit like a glove with the dominant ideas and policies of the New Labour Government in Britain and of neo-liberalism more generally: notions of health as individual responsibility, rejection of poverty and inequality as explanatory frameworks, an abhorrence of dependency in any form or the very specific policy announced by Works and Pensions Secretary John Hutton in July of this year to save billions of pounds by removing 1 million people from Incapacity benefit (*The Guardian*, 5 July 2006). In this context, should Layard's plans be implemented, one can only feel concern for those with mental health problems who, for whatever reason, have failed to attain good mental health after the prescribed 16 weeks of CBT.

'Another World is Possible!' The Challenge of the Anti-Capitalist Movement

A more thoroughgoing challenge to the values and priorities of neo-liberalism than that presented by the 'science of happiness' has come from the new global social movements which have emerged in recent years, principally the anti-capitalist (or global justice) movement, and also the movement against war and occupation in Iraq.

In Chapter 1, I outlined some of the ways in which these movements have developed since their birth in the mobilisations against the WTO Millennium Round in Seattle in 1999. What might be the significance for social work of these new movements against neo-liberalism and against war?

At the most general level, as we saw in Chapter 6, on several occasions over the past 100 years the social work profession has been able to renew itself – and to renew its commitment to social justice – through its contact with, and involvement in, the great social movements of the day. As I argued in that chapter, the radical social work movement of the 1970s, and the anti-oppressive practice to which it gave rise, did not fall out of the sky but rather grew out of the radicalisation of social workers by their contacts with the women's movement, the civil rights movement and the trade union struggles of the late 1960s and early 1970s (Thompson, 2002). More recently, as we saw in Chapter 5, some of the most significant contributions to social work theory, practice and service development have come from the 'new social welfare movements' which have emerged in the past twenty years, such as the disability movement and the mental health users' movement (Williams, 1992; Barnes, 1997).

Earlier anti-war movements have also impacted on social work, often through the direct involvement within them of leading members of the profession. Jane Addams, for example, one of the founders of social work in the USA, was also an anti-war activist who founded the Women's Peace Party in 1915 and chaired an international peace congress in Hague in the same year demanding an end to the First World War. Her actions led to letters in the respectable *Chicago Tribune* demanding that she be hanged from the nearest lamp-post (Reisch and Andrews, 2002: 44)! Another prominent social worker, Lillian Wald, was President of the American Union against Militarism, and in an interview with the *New York Evening Post* in December 1914 outlined her view of social work as follows:

> In its broadest conception, social work is teaching the sanctity of human life and ... the doctrine of the brotherhood of man.... The social workers of our time are dreaming a great dream and seeing a great vision of democracy.... War is the doom of all that has taken years to build up. (Cited in Reisch and Andrews, 2002: 42)

In each of these cases, social work theory and practice was radicalised through its contact with these movements, leading to new forms of practice (including advocacy and collective approaches), a desire for more equal relationships between workers and those who use services (often reflected in a critique of notions of professionalism) and a deepening and extension of social work's value base. So what can social work today learn from the new movements that have sprung up in the past few years? Three themes seem particularly relevant:

Unity in diversity. As discussed in the Chapter 7, much of Left politics in the 1990s was dominated by notions of identity and difference, often reflecting mistrust between those involved in resisting different aspects of oppression and exploitation. By contrast, one of the great breakthroughs of the Seattle demonstrations in 1999 was that they brought together very disparate groups of people, notably the Teamsters and the Turtle Kids – the trade unionists and the young environmentalists – as well as peace campaigners, socialists, feminists and many others. Whatever their past differences, on that demonstration they were united against the agenda of the WTO and the destruction which its neo-liberal policies were wreaking on the planet and its people:

> Togetherness was the theme of the labour rally – not only solidarity among workers of the world but of organised labour with everyone else. There were incredible sights of Teamster president James Hoffa sharing a stage with student anti-sweatshop activists, of Earth Firsters marching with Sierra Clubbers, and a chain of bare-breasted BGH-free Lesbian Avengers weaving through a crowd of machinists. (Doug Henwood, cited in Charlton, 2000: 8)

That 'unity in diversity' has been a feature of movement gatherings since then. Similarly, in the gatherings of social workers, students, academics and service users that have taken place in Britain in recent years and which will be discussed in more detail below, many different political and professional viewpoints and interests have been represented. However, a shared abhorrence of the ways in which market-based and authoritarian policies are undermining good social work practice has provided a basis for unity around issues such as opposition to the demonisation of young people and of asylum seekers, and to the fragmentation of social work by the incursion of the market. In addition, there has been a determination to find ways of involving service users as partners in the creation of new forms of social work, based on a shared recognition that neither workers nor service users benefit from services driven, not by social work values, but by competition and the need to keep down costs.

The centrality of values. Values of equality, diversity, social justice, opposition to war and, above all, the assertion that 'Our world is not a commodity' have been central to the building of the global justice movement. Discussion of the kind of values that are required for human beings to continue living on the planet in the decades to come has been an important feature of the literature of the movement (e.g. Albert, 2003; Callinicos, 2003; George, 2004). In contrast, as noted in Chapter 3, one of the main prongs of the neo-liberal attack on social work over the past two decades has been the attempt to excise or downgrade 'values talk' from social work education and practice, and to reconstruct social workers as social technicians or social engineers, carrying out ethically neutral tasks. Despite these attempts, it is above all the ways in which neo-liberal approaches, including the demonisation of certain social groups, are experienced as undermining core social work values that is creating dissatisfaction across broad layers of social workers and fuelling the call for a return to forms of social work rooted in social justice and social solidarity.

Creating our own forums. Once a year, the top businessmen, politicians and bureaucrats who make the key decisions concerning the future of the world economy, meet at the pleasant Swiss holiday resort of Davos to discuss how they can dismantle even more trade barriers and make even more profits out of the poor of the world. In response, every year since 2001 the global justice movement has held a World Social Forum at Porto Alegre in Brazil to look at how their plans can be resisted and alternatives developed which benefit the majority of the world's peoples. In recent years, World Social Forums have also been held in other locations including Mumbai and Caracas while Regional Forums have taken place in Europe, Cairo and elsewhere (Ashman, 2005).

Holding similar forums at local, national and international level will be an essential means through which social workers and service users can begin to develop new visions of what an engaged social work practice could be like. Sometimes such forums will be initiated by relevant trade unions, at other times by professional organisations, academic social work staff or loose networks such as the Social Work Action Network formed at a Glasgow Social Work Conference in 2007. What matters less is who convenes them but what matters more is that they provide a means of overcoming the isolation that so many workers currently feel and provide a space where debate and discussion over practice issues, such as the potential and dangers of direct payments (DPs) as a form of service delivery, can take place. In the next section, we will consider why these forums are necessary, and the form they might take.

'I Didn't Come into Social Work for This!'

In December 2004, around sixty social workers attended a meeting in Glasgow, Scotland on the theme 'I didn't come into social work for this.' That title reflected the dissatisfaction amongst these social workers at what their jobs had become, a dissatisfaction which, the research of the principal speaker at the meeting, Chris Jones of Liverpool University, suggested, was far from being confined to Glasgow. That meeting agreed to form a network based around a Manifesto for Social Work and Social Justice, which was drawn up by Jones and his colleagues. The Manifesto provided an analysis of the roots of social work's current crisis and also indicated possible 'resources of hope' for a more radical social work (Jones et al., 2004). Since then, almost 500 British social workers, social work academics and students have signed up to the Manifesto, and it has provided the basis for national conferences in Liverpool in 2006 and Glasgow in 2007 on the theme 'Social Work – a Profession Worth Fighting For?' (www.socialworkfuture.org). Significantly, shortly before the Liverpool Conference, and independently of it, a one-day conference also took place in Nottingham on the theme 'Affirming Our Value Base in Social Work and Social Care', addressed by some of the best-known critical social work academics in the UK and attended by almost 2,000 participants (Beresford, 2006).

In Chapters 1 and 3, I have pointed to some of the roots of this widespread dissatisfaction with the current state of social work in the UK. They lie primarily in the way that the knowledge base, skills and values of professional social work have been distorted and undermined by the imposition since the early 1990s of a managerialist regime, driven by competition and market disciplines. As we saw in Chapter 3, one of the main effects of these changes since they were by the NHS and Community Care Act 1990 has been to hugely reduce the possibilities for social workers to undertake direct work with service users:

> Our [social workers'] contact with clients is more limited. It is in, do the assessment, get the package together, review after a spell and then close the case and get on with the next one as there were over 200 cases waiting an assessment. (Jones, 2004: 101)

This raises two issues. First, the changes described by Jones' respondent (and reported in *Changing Lives*, the Report of the 21st Century Review of Social Work in Scotland) flow mainly from the imposition of a care management model within the context of a social care market in which 'value for money' is the key priority (Harris, 2003). In other words, they relate directly to the extension of neo-liberal policies to social work and social care. Second, what Jones calls 'neo-liberal social work' undermines not just collective, community work approaches but also more traditional, relationship-based approaches, a point also made by Harris in his study of the transformation of social work over the past two decades (Harris, 2003).

As we saw in Chapter 3, a second factor fuelling worker dissatisfaction is the profound moral authoritarianism underpinning many of New Labour's social policies, especially in areas such as asylum seekers and youth justice (Butler and Drakeford, 2001). Such authoritarianism is the flip-side of New Labour's persistent emphasis on 'individual responsibility' and its habit of deriding any reference to the impact of poverty or alienation on individual behaviour as 'excuse-making'.

It is, then, these aspects of neo-liberal social work – its undermining not just of collective approaches but also of more traditional, relationship-based social work approaches, its authoritarian distaste for core social work values, as well as its preference for a 'social work of surfaces' over deeper explanations of behaviour (Howe, 1996) – that have combined to create a deep dissatisfaction amongst many workers and to provide one basis for the emergence of more holistic, more critical approaches.

Reclaiming Social Work

In their valuable study of the ways in which fifty-nine service users, carers and social workers throughout the UK viewed social work, based on interviews conducted during 2005, Cree and Davis uncovered not only a very positive view of the value of social work, based on personal experience, but also a high degree of consensus about what social work could offer (Cree and Davis, 2007). Thus, the carers and service users wanted practitioners who would listen to them, who would treat them with respect and who would see them in the context of their families and communities. They wanted emotional and material support to enable them to live independent lives, and they wanted flexible and responsive services. The practitioners whom they interviewed were also clear about the kind of profession they wanted to belong to. Most had entered social work either out of a desire to help others, or to challenge social injustice, or both. They wanted to work creatively with people, helping them to change their lives and perhaps make some changes in society as a whole. It was these aspirations more than anything that kept them going and kept them in the job (2007: 148).

Cree and Davis' findings mirror those of other social work studies, such as *Changing Lives* (Scottish Executive, 2006a), which similarly found that what social workers valued most about their jobs was the opportunity to work directly with people, to build what the Report called 'therapeutic relationships'. What *Changing Lives* also found, however, as have other researchers including Jones (2001), Huxley et al. (2005) and Cree and Davis themselves, was that the ways in which social work has changed in recent years means that the opportunities for working in this way have become increasingly limited, giving rise to frustration, disillusionment and even despair.

This sense of social work having lost its way is a crucial part of what is sometimes referred to as the crisis of social work (Lymbery, 2001).

In this book, building on the work of Harris, Jones and other writers in the critical and radical traditions, I have argued that the roots of this crisis are to be found in the ways in which social work, like other health and welfare professions, has been transformed over the past two decades by the imposition of a business culture which is inimical to the values and practices of social work. I have also suggested, however, that if the dissatisfaction which such neo-liberal social work is producing can be given a voice, and if it can be linked to those other forces in society which are also involved in resisting the devastating effects of these policies at a societal level, including movements against neo-liberalism and war, welfare movements of the type discussed in Chapter 5 and the trade unions, then there is hope. Part of that task involves *reclaiming* social work. This is likely to involve some, or all, of the following:

Reclaiming the ethical

As we saw in Chapter 3, the New Labour government's desire to create a social work 'fit' for the purposes which it envisages involves challenging social work's core values both directly (in areas such as asylum and youth justice) and also indirectly (e.g. through the imposition of a technicist, 'evidence-based' model of practice, and through de-emphasising the place of values within social work education). More than any other single factor, it has been the attacks on these core values, and the expectation that social workers will collude with policies that are perceived as harming service users, that has produced the greatest anger and resistance within the profession. One expression of that anger and resistance was the 'Affirming Our Value Base in Social Work and Social Care' Conference which took place in Nottingham in 2006. One experienced commentator described the Conference in the following way:

> There were about 2,000 people present. This is likely to become the stuff of legend. I have just never seen so many people together all heading in one direction, all come to find out more about how to do social work and social care well and make it the user-centred service it truly can be.... Some of social care's key moral guardians, like Bill Jordan, Bob Holman and Beatrix Campbell were there to inspire. They stressed the need for social care workers to be politically engaged. (Beresford, 2006)

A very similar atmosphere was evident at the subsequent Liverpool Conference on the theme 'A Profession Worth Fighting For?' (www. socialworkfuture.org). The recognition that both the subordination of social work skills to market values and the moral authoritarianism that scapegoats young people and asylum seekers are inimical to core social work values provides an important basis for resistance. As Webb has argued:

> We need to take steps to reawaken core ethical practices and activate the moral sources of social work, both within and without the profession. Using a British example, a very obvious instance of this might be for educators and practitioners to lobby the General Social care Council and national Occupational Standards bodies insisting on the reinstatement of social work ethics, as central rather than marginal to the prescribed curriculum of the new degree. (Webb, 2006: 233)

Reclaiming Relationship and Process

As noted earlier, a key finding of *Changing Lives* was the importance of 'therapeutic relationships' between social workers and individuals and families in achieving change. In their submission to the Review, McNeil et al., drawing on the person-centred approach of Carl Rogers (Rogers, 1961), identified three key components of successful interventions which lead to behavioural change:

- Accurate empathy, respect or warmth and therapeutic genuineness;
- Establishing a therapeutic relationship or working alliance (mutual understanding and agreement about the nature and purpose of intervention); and
- An approach that is person centred, or collaborative and client driven (taking the client's perspective and using the client's concepts). (Cited in Scottish Executive, 2006a: 27)

What the Report also found that it was precisely this aspect of their work that social workers felt that been devalued and eroded in recent years. Consequently, its authors argued that

> We must now legitimise and restore the centrality of working for change through therapeutic relationships as the basis for strengthening the profession for the 21st century. (Scottish Executive, 2006a: 28)

However one defines 'therapeutic', an emphasis on the worker/client relationship has historically been central to *all* forms of social work since its origins in the late nineteenth century, including more radical variants. In their seminal 1970s text, for example, Bailey and Brake argued that

> Our aim is not, for example, to eliminate casework, but to eliminate casework that supports ruling-class hegemony. To counteract the effects of oppression, the social worker needs to innovate a dual process, assisting people to understand their alienation in terms of their oppression, and building up their self-esteem. (Bailey and Brake, 1975: 9)

It is often through such relationship-based work that the psychological damage and internalised oppression which results from living in an oppressive and unequal society can be addressed, and a sense of self-respect and self-worth re-created. In our own research into the views and experiences of people with the label of personality disorder, the importance of trusting relationships as a basis for addressing the effects of past and present abuse was repeatedly emphasised by workers and service user respondents alike (Ferguson et al., 2003; 2005; Stalker et al., 2005).

> It's all about trust. Dr X listens to me, she understands what I'm saying. She's never let me down. (Service user respondent, quoted in Ferguson et al., 2003: 31)

Reclaiming the Social

Putting relationship back into social work is likely to receive widespread support from social workers of different ideological persuasions, for the reasons given above. At the same time, while worker/client relationships based on the elements outlined above need to underpin all forms of practice, the current rediscovery of the importance of 'therapeutic relationships' is not without its dangers. In a context where Reports such as *Changing Lives* see the primary role of social workers as being able to work with 'high-risk' individuals or families, there is a risk of a return to the very individualised, potentially pathologising models which predominated before the emergence of both radical and ecological social work.

In addition, while Fook and other critical social work theorists are understandably critical of strands within radical thinking in the 1970s and 1980s which presented collective or structural approaches as the *only* genuinely radical models (Fook, 2002), this is hardly the issue in the twenty-first century. In the UK at least, not only community work approaches but also group work and social networking approaches have all but disappeared from the social work curriculum (Ward, 2002). While direct, one-to-one work with individuals or families is one means of addressing the problems experienced by people using social work services, it is neither the only one, nor always the most appropriate one.

As an example, in the personality disorder study referred to above, several of the service user respondents identified loneliness as one of their biggest problems, arising from a variety of factors including their difficulties in forming relationships, the stigma of mental ill-health and local housing policies. Loneliness is a category which rarely appears in the psychiatric literature, yet a study carried out by the mental health charity MIND in 2004 showed that 84 per cent of people with mental health problems felt isolated (MIND, 2004). For our respondents, that loneliness often led them to resort to drug or alcohol misuse and in some cases was a contributory factor to the loss of their tenancy. Many of them did not, however, find individual approaches (in the form of one-to-one counselling) helpful since they felt unable to manage the feelings to which such counselling gave rise. In such situations, community development, social networking and social support approaches would often be a more appropriate response than individual work (Payne, 2005: 155–6). Reclaiming such approaches is an essential part of reclaiming social work, as ways of addressing the 'erosion of solidarity' which neo-liberal policies have created across so many working-class communities (Lorenz, 2005).

Reclaiming the Structural

One of the major achievements of the radical social work movement of the 1970s was to ensure that an understanding of the impact of structural factors be part of every social work student's professional education, through the inclusion of sociology in social work courses. That understanding has been diluted in recent years, in part due to changes in the social work curriculum which have highlighted skills and tasks at the expense of knowledge, in part due to an (initially valid) focus within some critical social work approaches on *individual* agency, increasingly displacing any concern either with *collective* agency or with the structural determinants of service users' lives, partly for reasons discussed in the Chapter 7. This is ironic, for while social work has been moving away from a concern with the structural, a range of theorists from other professional and academic backgrounds – psychology, health epidemiology, political science – having been developing increasingly sophisticated analyses of the way in which factors such as economic inequality shape every aspect of people's existence, including their sense of self, their ability to trust other people, the level of violence they are likely to experience and their life expectancy (see for example Sennet, 2004; Wilkinson, 2005; James, 2007). Reclaiming that structural understanding of society in the form of a critical sociology is an essential task in reconstructing a social work practice capable of grasping the totality of service users' lives (Simpson and Price, 2007).

Conclusion: Reclaiming the Political

In conclusion, while an ethical response to the destruction wreaked on the lives of service users by neo-liberal policies of the sort suggested earlier by Webb is an essential starting-point, an exclusive reliance on values as a basis for resistance also carries dangers. In the past, an emphasis on the ethical dimension of social work has sometimes acted as a substitute for rigorous critical analysis of social work's role within the State and society: in short, the *politics* of social work (Powell, 2001). In part, this is because the very vagueness and ambiguity of value terms like 'empowerment' or 'respect' make them vulnerable to appropriation by powerful forces inimical to social work values and objectives. As Butler and Drakeford have rightly observed in their discussion of British social work under

jargon can be hijacked

New Labour, there has been

> a very real cost in the flexible exploitation of ambiguity which has allowed social work to retain the semblance of loyalty to its own values, while carrying out the bidding of political masters with very different ideas and purposes. (Butler and Drakeford, 2001: 8)

On the one hand, this suggests the need for ethical responses to be underpinned by critical analyses of the political context in which social work is operating, of the type which I have attempted to provide in this book. On the other, it means that social workers need to be much more vocal, both about the way in which social policies are impacting on the lives of their clients and also about the value (as well as the limits) of their own role. Cree and Davis reach a similar conclusion in their study of the views of service users and workers:

> In thinking about social work in the future, a theme which stands out from the interviews is best summed up by the practitioner who said she felt that social work had been, to date, a 'quiet profession'. In this she reflected a view expressed by many of those whom we interviewed, that social work needs to stand up and be counted; we need to be much clearer about what social work can, and cannot, offer; we need to be willing to contribute to public debates about issues as diverse as offending and the impact of poverty on the lives of those using social work services. (2007: 159)

The evidence not only from their study but also from much of the research conducted into social work in recent years suggests that the aspiration to 'make a difference' continues to be the major reason why people are attracted to social work. Realising that aspiration in the current situation will require vision, confidence, organisation and not a little courage. If these things can be found, however, then social work can finally stop being a 'quiet profession' and can begin to play its proper role in the struggle for a more equal, more just society.

References

Acheso Report (1998) *Independent Inquiry into Inequalities in Health*, London: The Stationery Office.

Albert, M. (2003) *Parecon: Life after Capitalism*, London: Verso.

Ali, T. (2006) *Pirates of the Caribbean: Axis of Hope*, London: Verso.

Alinsky, S. (1973) *Rules for Radicals*, USA: Random House.

Allan, J., Pease, B. and Briskman, L. (eds) (2003) *Critical Social Work: An Introduction to Theories and Practices*, Australia: Allen and Unwin.

Allott, P. (2005) 'Recovery', in D. Sallah and M. Clark (eds) *Research and Development in Mental Health*, London: Churchill Livingstone.

Armstrong, P., Glyn, A. and Harrison, J. (1991) *Capitalism since 1945*, London: Blackwell.

Ashman, S. (2005) 'Where do we go from here?' in G. Hubbard and D. Miller (eds) *Arguments against G8*, London: Pluto Press.

Attlee, C. (1920) *The Social Worker*, London: Heinemann.

Audit Commission (2002) *Integrated Services for Older People*, London: Audit Commission.

Bailey, R. and Brake, M. (eds) (1975) *Radical Social Work*, London: Edward Arnold.

Baldwin, M. (2002) 'New Labour and Social Care: Continuity or Change?' in M. Powell (ed.) *Evaluating New Labour's Welfare Reforms*, Bristol: The Policy Press.

Barker, C. (1986) *Festival of the Oppressed: Solidarity, Reform and Revolution in Poland 1980–81*, London: Bookmarks.

Barnes, M. (1997) *Care, Communities and Citizens*, London: Longman.

Barnes, M. and Shardlow, P. (1996) 'Identity crisis: mental health user groups and the "problem" of identity', in C. Barnes and G. Mercer (eds) *Exploring the Divide: Illness and Disability*, Leeds: The Disability Press.

Barrett, M. and Phillips, A. (eds) (1992) *Destabilizing Theory: Contemporary Feminist Debates*, Cambridge: Polity Press.

Bassac (2006) 'Contract culture threatens community groups, research finds', Press release, 4 February 2006. www.bassac.org.uk (accessed 4 June, 2006).

Bauman, Z. (1988) *Freedom*, Buckingham: Open University Press.

Bauman, Z. (2005) *Work, Consumerism and the New Poor*, 2nd edn, Berkshire: Open University Press.

Beck, U. and Ritter, M. (1992) *Risk Society: Towards a New Modernity*, London: Sage.

Becker, S. (1997) *Responding to Poverty*, London: Longman.

Bentall, R. (2003) *Madness Explained: Psychosis and Human Nature*, London: Penguin.

Beresford, P. (2006) 'Nottingham meeting gladdens the heart', *Community Care*, 16 March, 2006.

Beresford, P. and Croft, S. (1993) *Citizen Involvement: A Practical Guide for Change*, London: Macmillan.

Beresford, P. and Croft, S. (1995) 'Whose empowerment? Equalising the competing discourses in community care', in R. Jack (ed.) *Empowerment in Community Care*, London: Chapman and Hall.

Beresford, P. and Croft, S. (2004) 'Service users and practitioners reunited: the key component for social work reform', *British Journal of Social Work*, 34(1): 53–68.

Berman, M. (1982) *All that is Solid Melts into Air: The Experience of Modernity*, London, Verso.

Bevan, A. (1952/1990) *In Place of Fear*, London: Quartet.

Blackburn, C. (1991) *Poverty and Health: Working with Families*, Buckingham: Open University Press.

Blair, T. (1998) *The Third Way*, London: The Fabian Society.

Blair, T. (2004) ' "Choice, excellence & equality" in public services', Speech on public services delivered at Guys and St Thomas' Hospital, London, on 23 June 2004. Full speech can be found on http://news.bbc.co.uk/1/hi/uk_politics/3833345. stm (accessed 5 August 2006).

Bowes, A. and Sim, D. (2006) 'Advocacy for Black and minority ethnic populations: understandings and expectations', *British Journal of Social Work*, 36(7): 1209–25.

Bradley, H. (2000) 'Social inequalities: coming to terms with complexity', in G. Browning, A. Haleli and F. Webster (eds) *Understanding Contemporary Society: Theories of the Present*, London: Sage.

Brandon, D. (1991) *Innovation without Change? Consumer Power in Psychiatric Services*, Basingstoke: Macmillan.

Branfield, F. and Beresford, P. (2006) *Making User Involvement Work: Supporting Service User Networking and Knowledge, Findings*, York: Joseph Rowntree Foundation.

Braye, S. and Preston-Shoot, M. (1995) *Empowering Practice in Social Care*, Buckingham: Open University Press.

Brewer, C. and Lait, J. (1980) *Can Social Work Survive?*, London: Temple Smith.

Briskman, L. (2003) 'Indigenous Australians: towards postcolonial social work', in J. Allan, B. Pease and L. Briskman (eds) *Critical Social Work: An Introduction to Theories and Practices*, Australia: Allen and Unwin.

Broadie, A. (ed.) (1997) *The Scottish Enlightenment: An Anthology*, Edinburgh: Canongate.

Brown, G. and Harris, T. (1978) *Social Origins of Depression: A Study of Psychiatric Disorder in Women*, London: Tavistock.

Browning, G., Halcli, A. and Webster, F. (eds) (2000) *Understanding Contemporary Society: Theories of the Present*, London: Sage.

Burkett, I. and McDonald, C. (2004) 'Working in a different space: linking social work and social development', in I. Ferguson, M. Lavalette and E. Whitmore (eds) *Globalisation, Global Justice and Social Work*, London: Routledge.

Burr, V. (2003) *Social Constructionism*, 2nd edn, London: Routledge.

Burrows, R. and Loader, B. (eds) (1994) *Towards a Post-Fordist Welfare State?*, London: Routledge.

Butler, I. and Drakeford, M. (2001) 'Which Blair project? communitarianism, social authoritarianism and social work', *Journal of Social Work*, 1(1): 7–19.

Callinicos, A. (1989) *Against Postmodernism*, Cambridge: Polity Press.

Callinicos, A. (1999) *Social Theory: A Historical Introduction*, Cambridge: Polity Press.

Callinicos, A. (2000) *Equality*, Cambridge: Polity Press.

Callinicos, A. (2001) *Against the Third Way: An Anti-Capitalist Critique*, Cambridge: Polity Press.

Callinicos, A. (2003) *The New Mandarins of American Power*, Cambridge: Polity Press.

Campbell, P. (1996) 'The history of the user movement in the United Kingdom', in T. Heller, J. Reynolds, R. Gomm, R. Muston and S. Pattison (eds) *Mental Health Matters: A Reader*, Basingstoke: Macmillan.

Carmichael, A. and Brown, L. (2002) 'The future challenge for direct payments', *Disability and Society*, 17(7): 797–808.

Carpenter, M. (1994) *Normality is Hard Work: Trade Unions and the Politics of Community Care*, London: Lawrence and Wishart.

Carr, S. (2004) *Has Service User Participation Made a Difference to Social Care Services?* SCIE Position Paper No. 3, Summary, London: SCIE.

Carvel, J. (2000) 'Welfare reform: special report', *The Guardian*, 17 July 2000.

CEPMHPG (2006) *The Depression Report: A New Deal for Depression and Anxiety Disorders*, London: Centre for Economic Performance's Mental Health Policy Group, London School of Economics and Political Science.

Chamberlin, J. (1988) *On Our Own*, London: MIND Publications.

Charities Commission (2007) *Stand and Deliver: The Future for Charities Delivering Public Services*, London: Charities Commission.

Charlton, J. (1999) *It Just Went Like Tinder: The Mass Movement and New Unionism in Britain 1889*, London: Redwords.

Charlton, J. (2000) 'Talking Seattle', *International Socialism*, 86: 3–18.

Cigno, K. (2002) 'Cognitive-behavioural practice' in R. Adams, L. Dominelli and M. Payne (eds) *Social Work: Themes, Issues and Critical Debates*, 2nd edn, London: Palgrave Macmillan.

Clark, H., Gough, H. and McFarlane, A. (2004) *It Pays Dividends: Direct Payments and Older People*, Bristol: Policy Press.

Clarke, J. (ed.) (1993) *A Crisis in Care? Challenges to Social Work*, London: Sage.

Clarke, J. (1996) 'After social work?' in N. Parton (ed.) *Social Theory, Social Change and Social Work*, London: Routledge.

Clarke, J. (2004) *Changing Welfare, Changing States: New Directions in Social Policy*, London: Sage.

Clarke, J. and Newman, J. (1997) *The Managerialist State*, London: Sage.

Cliff, T. and Gluckstein, D. (1988) *The Labour Party: A Marxist History*, London: Bookmarks.

Cooke, I. (1996) 'Whatever happened to the class of '68? – The changing context of radical community work' in I. Cooke and M. Shaw (eds) *Radical Community Work: Perspectives from Practice in Scotland*, Edinburgh: Moray House Publications.

Corrigan, P. and Leonard, P. (1978) *Social Work under Capitalism: A Marxist Approach*, London: Macmillan.

Craig, C. (2003a) *The Scots' Crisis of Confidence*, Edinburgh: Big Thinking.

Craig, C. (2003b) *An Attitude Problem*, Edinburgh: Holyrood.

Cree, V. and Davis, A. (2007) *Social Work: Voices from the Inside*, London: Routledge.

Crook, S. (1990) '"The end of radical social theory?" Notes on radicalism, modernism and postmodernism' in R. Boyne and A. Rattansi (eds) *Postmodernism and Society*, London: Macmillan.

Curtis, P. (2006) 'NHS study questions use of new schizophrenia drugs', *The Guardian*, 24 November, 2006.

Dalrymple, J. and Burke, B. (1995) *Anti-Oppressive Practice: Social Care and the Law*, Buckingham: Open University Press.

Danaher, K. (ed.) (2001) *Democratizing the Global Economy*, Philadelphia, PA: Common Courage Press.

Davies, N. (1998) *Dark Heart: The Shocking Truth about Hidden Britain*, London: Vintage.

Davies, S. (2006) *Third Sector Provision of Employment-Related Services*, London: PCS.

Davis, A. (2005) 'Service user involvement in mental health research and development' in D. Sallah and M. Clark (eds) *Research and Development in Mental Health*, London: Churchill Livingstone.

Davis, A. and Garrett, P.M. (2004) 'Progressive practice for tough times: social work, poverty and division in the twenty-first century', in M. Lymbery and S. Butler (eds) *Social Work Ideals and Practice Realities*, Basingstoke: Macmillan.

Dean, M. (2005) 'Fears of the Leviathan', *The Guardian*, 9 March 2005.

Department of Health (1998) *Modernising Social Services*, London: The Stationery Office.

Department of Health (2005) *Tackling Health Inequalities: Status Report on the Programme for Action*, Scientific Reference Group on Health Inequalities, London: The Stationery Office.

Department of Health (2006) *Our Health, Our Care, Our Say: A New Direction for Community Services*, London: The Stationery Office.

Dominelli, L. (1997) *Anti-Racist Social Work*, London: Palgrave Macmillan.

Dominelli, L. (2002) 'Anti-oppressive practice in context', in R. Adams, L. Dominelli and M. Payne (eds) *Social Work: Themes, Issues and Critical Debates*, 2nd edn, London: Palgrave Macmillan.

Dominelli, L. (2003) *Anti-Oppressive Social Work Theory and Practice*, Basingstoke: Macmillan.

Dominelli, L. and McLeod, E. (1989) *Feminist Social Work*, London: Palgrave Macmillan.

Donzelot, J. (1980) *The Policing of Families: Welfare versus the State*, London: Hutcheson.

Douglas, A. (1999) 'Political correctness: myth or reality?' in T. Philpot (ed.) *Political Correctness and Social Work*, London: IEA.

Elliot, G. (1993) *Labourism and the English Genius*, London: Verso.

England, H. (1986) *Social Work as Art: Making Sense for Good Practice*, London: Harper Collins.

European Commission (2004) *Proposal for a Directive of the European Parliament and the Council on Services in the Internal Market*. 5 March COM (2004) Final/3, Brussels.

Faulkner, A. et al. (2002) *Being There in a Crisis: A Report of the Learning from Eight Mental Health Crisis Centres*, London: Mental Health Foundation/The Sainsbury Centre for Mental Health.

Ferguson, I. (1994) 'Containing the crisis: crime and the Tories', *International Socialism*, 62: 51–70.

Ferguson, I. (1999) *The Potential and Limits of Mental Health Service User Involvement*, unpublished PhD Thesis, University of Glasgow.

Ferguson, I. (2000) 'Identity politics or class struggle? The case of the mental health users' movement', in M. Lavalette and G. Mooney (eds) *Class Struggle and Social Welfare*, London: Routledge.

Ferguson, I. (2003) 'Mental health and social work', in D. Baillie, K. Cameron, L.-A. Cull, J. Roche and J. West (eds) *Social Work and the Law in Scotland*, Basingstoke: Palgrave Macmillan/OU.

Ferguson, I. (2005) *Involving Service Users and Carers in Social Work Education: Evaluation Report of the Dundee Demonstration Project*, Scottish Institute for Excellence in Social Work Education, www.sieswe.org/docs/IA33EvalDemo.pdf

Ferguson, I. (2006) 'An attitude problem? Mental health, inequality and "the science of happiness"', *Health Inequalities and Social Work ESRC Seminar Series*, University of Coventry.

Ferguson, I. (2007) 'Increasing user choice or privatizing risk? The antinomies of personalization', *British Journal of Social Work*, Special Issue on Adult Care, April 2007.

Ferguson, I. and Barclay, A. (2002) *Seeking Peace of Mind: The Mental Health Needs of Asylum Seekers in Glasgow*, University of Stirling (www.dass.stir.ac.uk) (accessed 10 February 2007).

Ferguson, I. and Lavalette, M. (1999) 'Social work, postmodernism and Marxism', *European Journal of Social Work*, 2(1): 27–40.

Ferguson, I. and Lavalette, M. (2004) 'Beyond power discourse: alienation and social work', *British Journal of Social Work*, 34(3): 297–312.

Ferguson, I., Lavalette, M. and Mooney, G. (2002) *Rethinking Welfare: A Critical Perspective*, London: Sage.

Ferguson, I., Petrie, M. and Stalker, K. (2005) *Developing Accessible Services for Homeless People with Severe Mental Distress and Behavioural Difficulties*, University of Stirling (www.dass.stir.ac.uk) (accessed 10 February 2007).

Fook, J. (2002) *Social Work: Critical Theory and Practice*, London: Sage.

Foucault, M. (1967) *Madness and Civilisation*, New York: Pantheon Books.

Foucault, M. (1981) *The History of Sexuality, I*, Harmondsworth: Penguin.

Fraser, N. (1995) 'From recognition to redistribution? Dilemmas of justice in a "post-socialist" Age', *New Left Review* 212: 68–93.

Fraser, N. (2000) 'Rethinking recognition', *New Left Review* (New Series), 3: 107–20.

Fritz, T. (2004) *Transforming Europe into a Special Economic Zone: The EU's Service Directive*. www.spectrezine.org/europe/Fritz-vs-Bolkestein-EN.pdf (accessed 10 January 2007).

Fukuyama, F. (1993) *The End of History and the Last Man*, London: Penguin.

Fukuyama, F. (2007) *After the Neo-Cons: America at the Crossroads*, London: Profile Books.

Fyvell, T.R. (1961) *The Insecure Offenders: Rebellious Youth in the Welfare State*, London: Chatto and Windus.

Galloway, G. (2003) 'Palestine', in F. Reza (ed.) *Anti-Imperialism: A Guide for the Movement*, London: Bookmarks.

Garret, P.M. (2003) 'The trouble with Harry: Why the "new agenda of life politics" fails to convince', *British Journal of Social Work*, 33(3): 381–97.

George, S. (2004) *Another World Is Possible If…*, London: Verso.

Giddens, A. (1998) *The Third Way*, Cambridge: The Polity Press.

Giddens, A. and Diamond, P. (eds) (2005) *The New Egalitarianism*, London: Polity.

Glasby, J. and Beresford, P. (2006) 'Who knows best? Evidence-based practice and the service user contribution', *Critical Social Policy*, 26(1): 268–84.

Gordon, D. (2000) 'Inequalities in income, wealth and standard of living in Britain', in C. Pantazis and D. Gordon (eds) *Tackling Inequalities*, Bristol: The Policy Press.

Gramsci, A. (1978) *Selections from Political Writings 1921–1926*, edited by Quentin Hoare, London: Lawrence and Wishart.

Gray, M. and McDonald, C. (2006) 'Pursuing good practice? The limits of evidence-based practice', *Journal of Social Work*, 6(1): 7–20.

Griffiths, R. (Sir Roy) (1988) *Community Care: Agenda for Action* (The Griffiths Report), London: HMSO.

Grover, C. (2006) 'Welfare reform, accumulation and social exclusion in the United Kingdom', *Social Work and Society*, 4(1). www.socwork.net/2006/2/articles/grover (accessed 10 December 2006).

Gutch, R. (2005) 'The third-sector way', *The Guardian*, 2 November 2005.

Habermas, J. (1987) *The Philosophical Discourse of Modernity*, Cambridge: Polity.

Hanlon, P., Walsh, D. and Whyte, B. (2006) *Let Glasgow Flourish: A Comprehensive Report on Health and Its Determinants in Glasgow and West Central Scotland*, Glasgow: Glasgow Centre for Population Health.

Hanmer, J. and Statham, D. (1988) *Women and Social Work: Towards a More Woman-Centred Practice*, Basingstoke: Macmillan.

Hardy, B. and Wistow, G. (1999) 'Changes in the private sector', in B. Hudson (ed.) *The Changing Role of Social Care*, London: Jessica Kingsley Press.

Harman, C. (1984) *Explaining the Crisis: A Marxist Re-appraisal*, London: Bookmarks.

Harman, C. (1988) *The Fire Last Time: 1968 and After*, London: Bookmarks.

Harman, C. (2001) 'Beyond the boom', *International Socialism*, 90: 41–69.

Harris, J. (2003) *The Social Work Business*, London: Sage.

Harris, J. (2004) 'Consumerism: social development or social delimitation?' *International Social Work*, 47(4): 533–42.

Harris, J. (2006) 'Working in the social work business'. Speech at 'Social work: a profession worth fighting for?', Conference, University of Liverpool, 7/8 April 2006, MP3 file downloadable from www.socialworkfuture.org (accessed 4 November 2006).

Harrison, R. (2004) *The Life and Times of Sydney and Beatrice Webb 1858–1905: The Formative Years*, London: Palgrave Macmillan.

Hartnell, M. (1998) 'Kilbrandon and the Kilkenny cats', in M. Barry and C. Hallett (eds) *Social Exclusion and Social Work: Issues in Theory, Policy and Practice*, London: Russell House.

Harvey, D. (2005) *A Brief History of Neoliberalism*, Oxford: Oxford University Press.

Hayes, D. and Humphries, B. (eds) (2003) *Social Work, Immigration and Asylum: Debates, Dilemmas and Ethical issues for Social Work and Social Care*, London: Jessica Kingsley Publishers.

Healy, K. (2000) *Social Work Practices: Contemporary Perspectives on Change*, London: Sage.

Healy, K. (2005) *Social Work Theories in Contest: Creating Frameworks for Practice*, Basingstoke: Macmillan.

Herman, A. (2001) *The Scottish Enlightenment: The Scots' Invention of the Modern World*, London: Fourth Estate.

Hills, J. and Stewart, K. (eds) *A More Equal Society? New Labour, Poverty, Inequality, and Exclusion*, Bristol: Policy Press.

Holman, B. (1998) *Faith in the Poor*, London: Lion Hudson.

Holmes, J. (2002) 'All you need is cognitive behaviour therapy?', *British Medical Journal*, 324: 288–94.

Hope, T. (2004) 'Pretend it works: evidence and governance in the evaluation of the reducing burglary initiative', *Criminology and Criminal Justice*, 4(3): 287–308.

Howe, D. (1996) 'Surface and depth in social work practice', in N. Parton (ed.) *Social Theory, Social Change and Social Work*, London: Routledge.

Hubbard, G. and Miller, D. (eds) (2005) *Arguments Against G8*, London: Pluto Press.

Hughes, B. (1995) *Older People and Community Care: Critical Theory and Practice*, Buckingham: Open University Press.

Huxley, P., Evans, S., Gately, C., Webber, M. et al. (2005) 'Stress and pressures in mental health social work: the worker speaks', *British Journal of Social Work*, 35(7): 1063–79.

James, O. (2007) *Affluenza*, London: Vermillion.

Jay, M. (1996) *The Dialectical Imagination: A History of the Frankfurt School and the Institute of Social Research, 1923–1950*, Berkeley, CA: University of California Press.

Johnson, P., Wistow, G., Schulz, R. and Hardy, B. (2003) 'Interagency and interprofessional collaboration in community care: the interdependence of structures and values', *Journal of Interprofessional Care*, 17(1): 70–83.

Jones, C. (1983) *State Social Work and the Working Class*, London: Routledge and Kegan Paul.

Jones, C. (2004) 'The neo-liberal assault: voices from the front-line of British social work', in I. Ferguson, M. Lavalette and E. Whitmore (eds) *Globalisation, Global Justice and Social Work*, London: Routledge.

Jones, C. and Novak, T. (1993) 'Social work today', *British Journal of Social Work*, 23(3): 95–212.

Jones, C. and Novak, T. (1999) *Poverty, Welfare and the Disciplinary State*, London: Routledge.

Jones, C., Ferguson, I., Lavalette, M. and Penketh, L. (2004) *Social Work and Social Justice: A Manifesto for a New Engaged Practice*. www.liv.ac.uk/sspsw/manifesto (accessed 12 February 2007).

Jordan, B. and Jordan, C. (2000) *Social Work and the Third Way: Tough Love as Social Policy*, London: Sage.

Katz, C. (2005) 'Latin America's new "left" governments', *International Socialism*, 107: 145–63.

Keegan, W. (1984) *Mrs Thatcher's Economic Experiment*, London: Penguin.

Kestenbaum, A. (1999) *What Price Independence? Independent Living and People with High Support Needs*, Bristol: Policy press.

Kilbrandon Report (1965) *Children and Young People in Scotland* (Cmnd 2306), Edinburgh HMSO.

Knapp, M., Hardy, B. and Forder, J. (2001) 'Commissioning for quality: ten years of social care markets in England', *Journal of Social Policy*, 20: 283–306.

Kotowicz, Z. (1997) *R.D. Laing and the Paths of Anti-Psychiatry*, London: Routledge.

Kumar, K. (1995) *From Post-Industrial to Post-Modern Society: New Theories of the Contemporary World*. Oxford: Blackwell.

Kurlansky, M. (2004) *1968: The Year That Rocked the World*, London: Jonathan Cape.

Kuruvilla, S. (2004) 'Social work and social development in India', in I. Ferguson, M. Lavalette and E. Whitmore (eds) *Globalisation, Global Justice and Social Work*, London: Routledge.

Langan, M. (1993) 'The rise and fall of social work', in J. Clarke (ed.) *A Crisis in Care? Challenges to Social Work*, London: Sage.

Langan, M. (2002) 'The legacy of radical social work', in R. Adams, L. Dominelli and M. Payne (eds) *Social Work: Themes, Issues and Critical Debates*, London: Palgrave/Open University.

Langan, M. and Clarke, J. (1994) 'Managing in the mixed economy of care', in J. Clarke, A. Cochrane and E. McLaughlin (eds) *Managing Social Policy*, London: Sage.

Langan, M. and Day, L. (eds) (1992) *Women and Social Work: Issues in Anti-Discriminatory Practice*, London: Routledge.

Langan, M. and Lee, P. (1989) 'Whatever happened to radical social work?', in M. Langan and P. Lee (eds) *Radical Social Work Today*, London: Unwin Hyman.

Lansley, S. (2006) *Rich Britain: The Rise and Rise of the Super-Wealthy*, London: Politico's.

Lash, S. and Urry, J. (1987) *The End of Organised Capitalism*, Cambridge: Polity.

Lavalette, M. and Ferguson, I. (eds) (2007a) *International Social Work and the Radical Tradition*, London: Venture Press.

Lavalette, M. and Ferguson, I. (2007b) 'Democratic language and neo-liberal practice: the problem with civil society', *International Social Work*, 50(4): 447–59.

Lavalette, M. and Mooney, G. (1999) 'New Labour, new moralism; the welfare politics and ideology of New Labour under Blair', *International Socialism*, 85: 27–47.

Lavalette, M. and Mooney, G. (eds) (2000) *Class Struggle and Social Welfare*, London: Routledge.

Layard, R. (2005) *Happiness: Lessons from a New Science*, London: Penguin Books.

Leadbetter, D. (2004) *Personalisation through Participation: A New Script for Public Services*, London: Demos.

Leadbetter, D. and Lownsbrough, H. (2005) *Personalisation and Participation: The Future of Social Care in Scotland*, London: Demos.

Leece, J. (2004) 'Money talks but what does it say? Direct payments and the commodification of care', *Practice*, 16(3): 211–21.

Leonard, P. (1975) 'Towards a paradigm for radical practice', in R. Bailey and M. Brake (eds) *Radical Social Work*, London: Edward Arnold.

Leonard, P. (1984) *Personality and Ideology: Towards a Materialist Understanding of the Individual*, London: Routledge.

Leonard, P. (1997) *Postmodern Welfare: Reconstructing an Emancipatory Project*. London, Sage.

Levick, P. (1992) 'The Janus face of community care legislation: an opportunity for radical possibilities?' *Critical Social Policy*, 12(1): 75–92.

Levitas, R. (2000) 'Discourses of risk and utopia', in B. Adam, U. Beck and J. van Loon (eds) *The Risk Society and Beyond: Critical Issues for Social Theory*, London: Sage.

Lewis, J. (1995) *The Voluntary Sector, the State and Social Work in Britain*, Aldershot: Edward Elgar.

Lewis, S. (2005) *Direct Payments: Answering Frequently Asked Questions*, London: SCIE.

Lindow, V. (1995) 'Power and rights: the psychiatric system survivor movement', in R. Jack (ed.) *Empowerment in Community Care*, London: Chapman and Hall.

Lorenz, W. (1994) *Social Work in a Changing Europe*, London: Routledge.

Lorenz, W. (2005a) 'Social work and a new social order – challenging neoliberalism's erosion of social solidarity', *Social Work and Society*, 3(1): 2005. www.socwork.net/lorenz2005.pdf (accessed 1 September 2005).

Lorenz, W. (2005b) 'Social work and the Bologna process', *Social Work and Society*, 3(2): 2005. www.socwork.net/lorenz2005.pdf (accessed 20 January 2007).

Lymbery, M. (2001) 'Social work at the crossroads', *British Journal of Social Work*, 31(3): 369–84.

Lyotard, J.F. (1984) *The Postmodern Condition: A Report on Knowledge*, Manchester: Manchester University Press.

McDonald, C. (2006) *Challenging Social Work: The Context of Practice*, London: Palgrave.

McLaren, P. and Leonard, P. (eds) (1993) *Paulo Freire: A Critical Encounter*, London: Routledge.

McLean, U. (1989) *Dependent Territories: The Frail Elderly and Community Care*, London: NPHT.

McPherson, S., Richardson, P. and Leroux, P. (eds) (2003) *Clinical Effectiveness in Psychotherapy and Mental Health: Strategies and Resources for the Effective Clinical Governance*, London: Karnac Books.

Martin, G. (2002) 'The voluntary and private sectors are one and the same', *The Guardian*, 16 January 2002.

Marx, K. (1845/1970) *The German Ideology*, London: Lawrence and Wishart.

Mayer, J.E. and Timms, N. (1970) *The Client Speaks: Working-class Impressions of Casework*, London: Routledge and Kegan Paul.

Mayo, M. (1994) *Communities and Caring: the Mixed Economy of Welfare*, Basingstoke: Macmillan.

Means, R., Lart, R. and Taylor, M. (1994) 'Quasi-markets and community care: towards user empowerment?' in W. Bartlett, C. Propper, D. Wilson and J. LeGrand (eds) *Quasi-Markets in the Welfare State*, Bristol: SAUS.

Meiksins Wood, E. (1986) *The Retreat from Class: A New 'True' Socialism*, London: Verso.

Midgley, J. (2001) 'Issues in international social work', *Journal of Social Work*, 1(1): 21–35.

Miliband, D. (2005) 'Does inequality matter?' in A. Giddens and P. Diamond (eds) *The New Egalitarianism*, London: Polity.

Mills, C. Wright (1959/2000) *The Sociological Imagination*, Oxford: Oxford University Press.

Milner, J. and O'Byrne, P. (2002) *Assessment in Social Work*, London: Palgrave Macmillan.

MIND (2004) *Not Alone? Isolation and Mental Distress*, London: MIND.

Monbiot, G. (2001) 'Introduction', in E. Bircham and J. Charlton, *Anti-Capitalism: A Guide to the Movement*, London: Bookmarks.

Mooney, G. (2000) 'Class and social policy', in G. Lewis, S. Gewirtz and S. Clarke (eds) *Rethinking Social Policy*, London: Sage.

Mooney, G. and Poole, L. (2004) 'A land of milk and honey? Social policy in Scotland after devolution', *Critical Social Policy*, 24(4): 458–83.

Mullaly, B. (1997) *Structural Social Work: Ideology, Theory and Practice*, 2nd edn, Oxford: Oxford University Press.

Murray, A. and German, L. (2005) *Stop the War: The Story of Britain's Biggest Mass Movement*, London: Bookmarks.

Murray, C. (2006) 'Normality and the Jowells'. www.craigmurray.co.uk/ archives/2006/02/normality_and_t.html (accessed 28 February, 2006).

Nelson-Jones, R. (2000) *Six Key Approaches to Counselling and Therapy*, London: Continuum.

Netten, A., Darten, R., Davey, V., Kendall, J., Knapp, M., Williams, J., Fernandez, J.L. and Forder, J. (2005) *Understanding Public Services and Markets: Summary Paper of the Report Commissioned by the King's Fund for the Care Services Inquiry*, London: PSSRU.

Norris, C. (2000) 'Post-modernism: a guide for the perplexed', in G. Browning, A. Halcli, and F. Webster (eds) *Understanding Contemporary Society: Theories of the Present*, London: Sage.

O'Brien, M. and Penna, S. (1998) *Theorising Welfare: Enlightenment and Modern Society*, London: Sage.

Office for National Statistics (2004) *Focus on Social Inequalities*, London: The Stationery Office.

Oliver, M. (1996) *Understanding Disability: From Theory to Practice*, Basingstoke: Macmillan.

Oliver, M. and Barnes, C. (1998) *Disabled People and Social Policy: From Exclusion to Inclusion*, London: Longman.

Oliver, M. and Campbell, J. (1996) *Disability Politics: Understanding Our Past, Changing Our Future*, London: Routledge.

Oliver, J., Huxley, P., Bridges, K. and Mohamad, H. (eds) (1996) *Quality of Life and Mental Health Services*, London: Routledge.

One Plus (2006) *One Plus and the Scottish Economy*. www.oneplus.org/social-economy/social-economy (accessed 10 January 2007).

Orme, J. (2001) 'Regulation or fragmentation? Directions for social work under New Labour', *British Journal of Social Work*, 31: 611–24.

Palmer, G., Carr, J. and Kenway, P. (2005) *Monitoring Poverty and Social Exclusion in the UK*, York: Joseph Rowntree Foundation.

Pantazis, C., Gordon, D. and Levitas, R.A. (eds) *Poverty and Social Exclusion in Britain: The Millenium Survey*, Briston: Policy press.

Parsloe, P. (ed.) (1999) *Risk Assessment in Social Care and Social Work*, London: Jessica Kingsley Publishers.

Parton, N. (ed.) (1996) 'Introduction', *Social Theory, Social Change and Social Work*, London: Routledge.

Parton, N. and O'Byrne, P. (2000) *Constructive Social Work: Towards a New Practice*, London: Palgrave Macmillan.

Payne, M. (1995) *Social Work and Community Care*, Basingstoke: Macmillan.

Payne, M. (2002) 'The role and achievements of a professional association in the late twentieth century: The British Association of Social Workers 1970–2000', *British Journal of Social Work*, 32(8): 969–95.

Payne, M. (2005) *Modern Social Work Theory*, 3rd edn, Basingstole: Palgrave Macmillan.

Pearson, G. (1983) *Hooligans: A History of Respectable Fears*, London: Palgrave Macmillan.

Pearson, G. (1989) 'Women and men without work: the political economy is personal', in C. Rojek, G. Peacock and S. Collins (eds) *The Haunt of Misery: Critical Essays in Social Work and Helping*, London: Routledge.

Pease, B. and Fook, J. (eds) (1999) *Transforming Social Work Practice: Postmodern Critical Perspectives*, London: Routledge.

Pedersen, S. (2004) *Eleanor Rathbone and the Politics of Conscience*, Yale, CT: Yale University Press.

Peile, C. and McCouat, M. (1997) 'The rise of relativism: the future of theory and knowledge development in social work', *British Journal of Social Work*, 23(3): 343–60.

Penketh, L. (2001) *Tackling Institutional Racism*, Bristol: Policy Press.

Penna, S. (2004) 'Policy contexts of social work in Britain: the wider implications of "New" Labour and the "New Legal regime"', *Social Work & Society*, 1(1): 1–21.

Philpot, T. (ed.) (1999) *Political Correctness and Social Work*, London: IEA Health and Welfare Unit.

Pidd, H. (2006) 'A little more conversation', *The Guardian*, 30 June 2006.

Pilgrim, D. (2000) 'The real problem for postmodernism', *Journal of Family Therapy*, 22(1): 6–23.

Pilgrim, D. and Rogers, A. (2002) *Mental Health and Inequality*, London: Palgrave Macmillan.

Pincus, A. and Minahan, A. (1973) *Social Work Practice: Model and Method*, Itasca, IL: Peacock.

Plumb, S. (2005) 'The social/trauma model: mapping the consequences of childhood sexual abuse and similar experiences', in J. Tew (ed.) (2005) *Social*

Perspectives in Mental Health: Developing Social Models to Understand and Work with Mental Distress, London: Jessica Kingsley Publishers.

Plummer, J. (2006) 'Businesses and charities are very similar these days', *The Guardian*, 8 November 2006.

Pollock, A. (2004) *NHS plc: The Privatisation of Our Health Care*, London: Verso.

Popper, K. (1945/2002) *The Open Society and Its Enemies*, Volumes 1 and 2, London: Routledge.

Powell, F. (2001) *The Politics of Social Work*, London: Sage.

Pratt, A. (2005) 'Neoliberalism and social policy', in M. Lavalette and A. Pratt (eds) *Social Policy: Theories, Concepts and Issues*, London: Sage.

Preston-Shoot, M. and Agass, D. (1990) *Making Sense of Social Work*, Basingstoke: Macmillan.

Rawls, J. (1999) *A Theory of Justice*, revised edition, Oxford: Oxford University Press.

Reisch, M. (2004) 'American exceptionalism and critical social work: a retrospective and prospective analysis' in I. Ferguson, M. Lavalette and E. Whitmore (eds) *Globalisation, Global Justice and Social Work*, London: Routledge.

Reisch, M. and Andrews, J. (2002) *The Road Not Taken: A History of Radical Social Work in the United States*, New York: Brunner-Routledge.

Reynolds, B. (1963/1991) *An Uncharted Journey*, 3rd edn, Silver Spring: NASW Press.

Robb, C. (2005) 'Charities are complementing not competing', *The Guardian*, 24 January 2005.

Rogers, A. and Pilgrim, D. (1991) 'Pulling down churches: accounting for the British Mental Health Users' Movement', *Sociology of Health and Illness*, 13(2): 129–48.

Rogers, A., Pilgrim, D. and Lacey, R. (1993) *Experiencing Psychiatry*, Basingstoke: Macmillan.

Rogers, C. (1961) *On Becoming a Person*, Boston, MA: Houghton Mifflin.

Romme, M. and Escher S. (eds) (1998) *Accepting Voices*, 2nd edn, London: Mind Publications.

Rose, N. (1999) *Powers of Freedom: Reframing Political Thought*, Cambridge: Cambridge University Press.

Rosengard, A. and Laing, I. (2001) *User Consultation on the Millan Report*, Edinburgh: Scottish Executive Equality Unit & Public Health Division.

Roszak, T. (1969) *The Making of a Counter Culture*, New York: Doubleday and Co.

Save the Children (2006) News release, 9 March 2006 – 'Blair betrays Britain's poorest children.' www.savethechildren.org.uk (accessed 10 April 2006).

Schorr, A. (1992) *The Personal Social Services: An Outside View*, York: Joseph Rowntree Foundation.

Scottish Executive (2006a) *Changing Lives: Report of the 21st Century Social Work Review*, Edinburgh: Scottish Executive.

Scottish Executive (2006b) *Scottish Executive Response to the Report of the 21st Century Social Work Review*, Edinburgh: Scottish Executive.

Scourfield, P. (2005) 'Implementing the Community Care (Direct Payments) Act: will the supply of personal assistants meet the demand and at what price?' *Journal of Social Policy*, 34(3): 469–88.

Seebohm Report (1968) *Report on the Committee on Local Authority and Allied Personal Social Services* (Cmnd 3703), London: HMSO.

Sefton, T. and Sutherland, H. (2005) 'Poverty and inequality under New Labour', in J. Hills and K. Stewart (eds) *A More Equal Society? New Labour, Poverty, Inequality, and Exclusion*, Bristol: Policy Press.

Seligman, Martin E.P. (2002) *Authentic Happiness*, New York: Simon and Schuster.

Sennet, R. (2003) *Respect: The Formation of Character in an Age of Inequality*, London: Penguin.

Shardlow, S. (1989) *The Values of Change in Social Work*, London: Routledge.

Shaw, M., Davey Smith, G. and Dorling, D. (2005) 'Health inequalities and new labour: how the promises compare with real progress', *British Medical Journal*, 330(10): 16–21.

Simpkin, M. (1983) *Trapped Within Welfare?* 2nd edn, Basingstoke: Macmillan.

Simpson, G. and Price, V. (2007) *Transforming Society? Social Work and Sociology*, Bristol: The Policy Press.

Smith, C. and White, S. (1997) 'Parton, Howe and postmodernity: a critical comment on mistaken identity', *British Journal of Social Work*, 27(2): 275–95.

Smith, S. (1994) 'Mistaken identity – or can identity politics liberate the oppressed?' *International Socialism*, 62: 3–50.

Spandler, H. (2004) 'Friend or foe? Towards a critical assessment of direct payments', *Critical Social Policy*, 24(2): 187–209.

Specht, H. and Vickery, M. (1977) *Integrating Social Work Methods*, London: Allen and Unwin.

Stalker, K., Paterson, L. and Ferguson, I. (2005) *'Someone to Talk to': A Study of Social Crisis Services*, Department of Applied Social Science, University of Stirling.

Stedman-Jones, G. (1971) *Outcast London*, Oxford: Clarendon.

Stevenson, O. (1989) *Age and Vulnerability: A Guide to Better Care*, London: Hodder Arnold.

Stiglitz, J. (2002) *Globalization and Its Discontents*, London: Penguin.

Stirk, P.M.R. (2000) *Critical Theory, Politics and Society*, London: Pinter.

Taylor, M. (2005) 'Top state schools colonised by middle classes', *The Guardian*, 10 October 2005.

Taylor-Gooby, P. (1997) 'In defence of second-best theory: state, class and capital in social policy', *Journal of Social Policy*, 26(2): 171–92.

Tew, J. (ed.) (2005) *Social Perspectives in Mental Health: Developing Social Models to Understand and Work with Mental Distress*, London: Jessica Kingsley Publishers.

Tew, J. (2006) 'Understanding power and powerlessness: towards a framework for emancipatory practice in social work', *Journal of Social Work*, 6(1): 33–51.

Thompson, N. (2002) 'Social movements, social justice and social work', *British Journal of Social Work*, 32(6): 711–22.

Thompson, N. (2006) *Anti-Discriminatory Practice*, 4th edn, London: Palgrave Macmillan.

Thomson, S. and Hoggett, P. (1996) 'Universalism, selectivism and particularism', *Critical Social Policy*, 46: 211–43.

Thornton, P. and Kirby, T. (2006) 'Boom and bust Britain', *The Independent*, 4 February 2006.

Timmins, N. (1996) *The Five Giants: A Biography of the Welfare State*, London: Fontana.

Townend, M. and Braithwaite, T. (2002) 'Mental health research – the value of user involvement', *Journal of Mental Health*, 11(2): 117–19.

Toynbee, P. (2006a) 'The fight against poverty is half-won. Now we need a radical plan,' *The Guardian*, 10 March 2006.

Toynbee, P. (2006b) 'We will never abolish poverty in a society shaped like this', *The Guardian*, 7 July 2006.

Toynbee, P. and Walker, D. (2001) *Did Things Get Better? An Audit of Labour's Successes and Failures*, London: Penguin.

Ungerson, C. (1997) 'Give them the money: is cash a route to empowerment?' *Social Policy and Administration*, 31(1): 45–53.

Ungerson, C. (2004) 'Whose empowerment and independence? A cross-national perspective on "cash for care" schemes', *Ageing and Society*, 24(2): 189–212.

UNICEF (2007) *Report Card 7: Child Poverty in Perspective: An Overview of Child Well-being in Rich Countries*, Florence: UNICEF.

UNISON (2006) *Our Health, Our Care, Our Say*, Comments on the white paper from a UNISON social care perspective, London: UNISON.

Walsh, K. (1995) 'Citizens and contracts', in R. Keat, N. Whitely and N. Abercrombie (eds) *The Authority of the Consumer*, London: Routledge.

Walton, R.G. (1975) *Women in Social Work*, London: Routledge and Keegan Paul.

Ward, D. (2002) 'Groupwork', in R. Adams, L. Dominelli and M. Payne (eds) *Social Work: Themes, Issues and Critical Debates*, 2nd edn, London: Palgrave Macmillan.

Warner, R. (1994) *Recovery from Schizophrenia: Psychiatry and Political Economy*, London: Routledge.

Watson, D. and West, J. (2006) *Social Work Process and Practice: Approaches, Knowledge and Skills*, Basingstoke: Palgrave Macmillan.

Watson, S. (2000) 'Foucault and the study of social policy', in G. Lewis, S. Gewirtz and S. Clarke (eds) *Rethinking Social Policy*, London: Sage.

Webb, S. (2006) *Social Work in a Risk Society: Social and Political Perspectives*, London: Palgrave Macmillan.

Webb, S.A. (2006) *Social Work in a Risk Society: Social and Political Perspectives*, London: Palgrave.

Whelan, R. (2001) *Helping the Poor: Friendly Visiting, Dole Charities and Dole Queues*, London: Civitas.

Whitehead, M., Townsend, P. and Davidson, N. (eds) (1992) *Inequalities in Health: The Black Report and the Health Divide*, London: Penguin.

Whitmore, E. and Wilson, M. (2000) *Seeds of Fire: Social Development in an Era of Globalism*, New York: The Apex Press.

Wilkinson, R. (2005) *The Impact of Inequality: How to Make Sick Societies Healthier*, New York: The New Press.

Williams, C. (1999) 'Connecting anti-racist and anti-oppressive theory and practice: retrenchment or reappraisal?' *British Journal of Social Work*, 29(2): 211–30.

Williams, F. (1992) 'Somewhere over the rainbow: universality and diversity in social policy', *Social Policy Review*, 4: 200–19.

Williams, F. (1996) 'Postmodernism, feminism and the question of difference', in N. Parton (ed.) *Social Theory, Social Change and Social Work*, London: Routledge.

Williams, R. (1975) *Keywords: A Vocabulary of Culture and Society*, Glasgow: Fontana.

Wilson, G. (1997) 'A postmodern approach to structured dependency theory', *Journal of Social Policy*, 26(3): 341–50.

Wolfreys, J. (2005) 'How France's referendum caught fire', *International Socialism*, 107: 9–19.

Yip, Kam-shing (2007) 'Tensions and dilemmas of social work education in China', *International Social Work*, 50(1): 93–105.

Young, J. (1999) *The Exclusive Society*, London: Sage.

Index